# Steve Mizerak's Pocket Billiards

## TIPS AND TRICK SHOTS

# Steve Mizerak's Pocket Billiards

## TIPS AND TRICK SHOTS

Steve Mizerak
with Joel H. Cohen

WINGS BOOKS
New York • Avenel, New Jersey

Copyright © 1982 by Steve Mizerak and Joel H. Cohen

This 1995 edition is published by Wings Books,
distributed by Random House Value Publishing, Inc.,
40 Engelhard Avenue, Avenel, New Jersey 07001,
by arrangement with Contemporary Books, Inc.

Random House
New York • Toronto • London • Sydney • Auckland

Photographs by Nick Sorrentino

Printed and bound in the United States of America

**Library of Congress Cataloging–in–Publication Data**

Mizerak, Steve, 1944–
 [Pocket billiards, tips, and trick shots]
 Steve Mizerak's pocket billiards tips and trick shots / Steve Mizerak with
Joel H. Cohen.
     p.    cm.
 Originally published: Chicago : Contemporary Books, c 1982.
 Includes index.
 ISBN 0–517–12332–0
 1. Pool (Game)    I. Cohen, Joel H.    II. Title.    III. Title: Pocket
billiards, tips, and trick shots.
 GV891.M693    1995
 794.7'3—dc20                                          94–38547
                                                          CIP

8  7  6  5  4  3  2  1

# Contents

# Introduction:
# "Just Showin' Off"
# *or* The 30 Seconds That
# Changed My Life

It wasn't a very good time in my life. Even though I was an established schoolteacher and successful pocket billiards player—with 50 major titles, including four U.S. Open championships, to my credit—somehow nothing was happening. At least nothing good. There were severe domestic and money problems, and I had the feeling I wasn't going anywhere but down. Then I got a phone call that changed my life.

The caller was Marty Blackman, a lawyer-agent who represents several big-name professional athletes in their business dealings. He told me that the agency for Miller Lite Beer wanted to audition some pocket pool players for a TV commercial, and he asked whether I'd be interested in trying out. Is Bo Derek beautiful? Does George Steinbrenner fire managers? "Sure," I said, and on the appointed day I went to the agency.

Three other players from the Professional Pool Players Association were there: Allen Hopkins, Pete Margo, and Ray Martin. On a pool table I can hold my own against them, but on this occasion I felt outclassed. First of all, each of them already had a copy of the script for the commercial, while I had nothing but my cue stick. The agency people gave me a script. I studied it as the other players went in for their respective screen tests. Then it was my turn.

I'd been on a few TV shows before, but this was different. I was being tested for something I wanted badly, a commercial that obviously could be a ticket to those old favorites, Fame and Fortune. So, while I wasn't actually in a cold sweat, I was plenty nervous. The others each spent a half hour inside; I took about three and a half hours to get it right. When the session was over I told myself I had absolutely no chance whatsoever of pocketing the job.

"You'll never believe it," Marty Blackman told me on the phone the next day. "They picked you." He was right; I didn't believe him. "Marty, I was in there three and a half hours," I protested. "The other guys took only half an hour."

"That's just the point," he said. "You were the one guy who could walk, talk, shoot pool, and sound convincing all together. That's why they let everybody else go so quickly and kept you over three hours."

I was so excited, I was almost speechless. Then, when the thought registered I knew there was work to do. My first task was to help the agency people design three trick shots that would look spectacular while keeping the focus on the sponsor's product. After spending about a month perfecting them, it was time to play for keeps. One morning at about dawn, a limousine took me to the Knickerbocker Bar and Grill, somewhere in New York's Greenwich Village. There were three pool tables in camera range along with six specially designed beer bottles.

To me, the job of shooting three trick shots and saying a few commercial words to go with them looked like a hanger, and I figured it was going to be a snap. Was I ever wrong!

We got to the bar and grill at about 7:00 a.m. I had a little breakfast, put on my TV clothes, and started work at about 8:30.

"We'll be here all day," Marty predicted.

"What?" I said. "I want to get out of here by noon!"

Well, it was a quarter to twelve before we got the first good take. Sometimes the shot went wrong; sometimes the timing; sometimes the words. I had trouble saying, "and even though." Finally the crew wrote the phrase on a card, and when it came time to utter it there must have been ten guys pointing to the sign: "and even though."

I probably did the last trick shot 70 times before I got it to their satisfaction. That's the famous one, where the cue ball sinks six balls on one stroke, the last ball dropping into the corner pocket after I lift a Miller Lite out of its way.

On a few attempts everything worked fine, except the last ball didn't go into the pocket.

When you're doing trick shots you usually pick up the cue ball and put it somewhere else on the table for the second trick. For the commercial, though, I had to let the cue ball stay where it was, and that was the toughest part of the whole thing.

On half the tries the shot worked fine, but I was interested in seeing whether or not the cue ball was going to bang the last one into the pocket, and I forgot to look into the camera.

The crew started moaning and groaning, "Let's do it. Come on, do it." It was midafternoon when I finally did it, complete with that sheepish, smart-alecky grin the director wanted. The crew cheered, both in relief and in sincerity, "Hey, this guy *can* do it." We finished at about 7:00 that night, and the rest, as the saying goes, is history.

The commercial, which has been a huge success, opened doors for me I hardly knew were there. I've been living in something of a fantasy land. I never got half the recognition from winning 50 major pocket billiard titles and being the number one name in the sport that I did from the commercial. Hundreds and hundreds of fan letters were just one piece of evidence. And I've been on loads of TV shows, John Davidson's and Merv Griffin's among them.

In other Miller commercials and off camera I hobnob with the likes of Billy Martin, Bubba Smith, Boom-Boom Geoffrion, and Rodney Dangerfield. A yearly reunion that Miller hosts is something out of fantasy land.

The "Just Showin' Off" TV commercial turned my life around and has made me as happy as a fly in a nudist colony.

In this book, I'll show *you* how to do the trick shot that made me, along with about two dozen other shots to amaze your friends and maybe separate them from their dollars.

The trick shots are in both simple and advanced categories. There are shots that only I do, shots that will enable you to win a bundle.

I'm assuming that readers of this book have some familiarity with pocket billiards, so I won't go into the ABCs, but I will give you tips on the basics of the game, from selecting equipment to developing strategy.

I'll concentrate on tips for five major pocket billiards games— 14:1, Eight-Ball, Nine-Ball, One-Pocket, and a new sensation, Seven-Ball.

And I'll teach you what I can about pool hustling.

Once on "To Tell the Truth" I impersonated a real estate man who prided himself on buying great parcels of property with no money down. The actual real estate man got one vote; the other imposter got one, and I got two. One of the panelists said about me, "He looks like he can con anything out of anybody."

I hope I can con you into expanding your pool skills, trying some trick shots, and having the time of your life at the pool table.

# Steve Mizerak's
# Pocket Billiards
## TIPS AND TRICK SHOTS

# 1

# Tips on Equipment

## TABLES

Since the pool table is going to be your playground or battlefield, depending on how seriously you take the game, you want it to be the best you can afford.

The way inflation is ballooning, you should expect to pay upward of $1,000 for a good table. Anything that costs less is probably not going to be good. The old saying that you get what you pay for is as true of pool tables as it is of automobiles. You don't get a Mercedes for the price of a Ford. And, of course, decorative touches add to the price.

In my opinion, the three best manufacturers of pool tables are Brunswick of Chicago; Gandy Industries of Macon, Georgia; and Leisure World of Covina, California. Each of these firms makes excellent tables.

Brunswick makes the best pool table for a commercial establishment; Leisure World, the best table for the home; and Gandy, possibly the best combination of a home and commercial table.

The environment you're planning to use the table in can help you make a choice. If it's going into a well-decorated, finished recreation room, a Leisure World table would be a good choice. If you're planning to put it in an unfinished basement, and you still want a good table, go with a Gandy.

I have a favorite model in each line, which I recommend for your consideration: Brunswick's Gold Crown, Gandy's Big G, and Leisure World's Trafalgar.

A table's playing surface is the feature that should interest you most. The three I mentioned have similar types of surfaces and play the best.

Brunswick's tables are virtually indestructible and should last a hundred years, provided they're taken care of. Gandy may not have the same longevity but is a good buy for the money, somewhat less costly than Brunswick. Leisure World's tables are the most intricately designed of the three, with carved legs and other fancy features, and therefore are slightly more expensive than Brunswick.

Keep in mind that part of the price you're quoted is for installation (say, $250 out of the $1,495 you might pay for a table). It's worth the price because installation is a very difficult job.

## Let a Pro Do It

Don't—repeat, don't—install the table yourself. First of all, you could injure yourself, hauling and shoving a piece of furniture that can weigh a ton. Second, should you break any part of it, you'd be responsible. If you cracked the slate, for instance, what would you do? You wouldn't know how to fix it. Getting a professional to install the table, though it's going to cost you some money, is an excellent protection of your investment. If anything goes wrong, the installer or his firm is responsible for correcting it. And he'll do the extras, like applying the head and foot spots in a neat, professional way.

I donated a table to a Miller-sponsored project called Sky Ranch for Boys. Father Dale, the director of the facility, which is located about 50 miles from nowhere in the Dakotas, tried to assemble the table himself. He put it together backward. The boys were able to play on it for a while, but it wasn't long before the table was falling apart. So I told him to let it alone and we'd get a professional from the nearest city to fix it for him. "Father," I said, "you can pray pretty good, but you can't fix pool tables."

You're not going to have a telephone repairman fix your car; don't install your table yourself. Similarly, leveling the table is the expert's job. If a table's three slates are not. lined up properly, the table is going to have a roll, and once you correct one roll you're likely to develop another.

Some tables, such as Brunswick's Gold Crown, have leveling devices on the bottom of their legs. If your table doesn't, and you want to level it, all you have to do is use common sense and slip a matchbook cover or other thin piece of cardboard under the leg of the corner that needs elevating.

Once your slate table is in place, don't try to move it, because you're liable to strain your back and crack the slate or the floor on which the table is standing.

## Judging a Table

People ask how they can judge whether or not a table is solid. The answer is simple: bump it. If the table shakes and the balls move or shake, it's not solid. It's too light, and it's just not going to hold up. The heavier the table, the better.

## Used Tables

Used tables nowadays are almost as expensive as new ones, so rather than buy someone else's headache you'd do better to buy new, unless you pick up a good used table at a super price. If it's a meager $400 or $500, okay; otherwise, buy a new one.

There are exceptions to this piece of advice. I was playing golf at the Shackamaxon Country Club in New Jersey and happened to see a filthy old pool table stored away with some other junk. I wasn't interested until the following week when I saw an identical Lion's Head table at a sports show. The antique had an asking price of $12,000! I couldn't wait to get back to the country club to make a bid on the twin that was stored away. I would have offered $3,000, had it transported away, and restored and then sold it at a handsome profit. But it was gone.

## Trying Out a Table

Every table has its own "personality," and a pro will shoot on it to test it. He'll shoot a few balls down the rail and knock a few into the side pockets hard to check out the pockets.

You can try out a table, too, but, truthfully, unless you're an experienced player you probably aren't going to know what you're looking for.

## A Table's Dimensions

For a professional pool player the best size for a table is 4½ feet by 9 feet. It gives you ample room, and games take longer. But the shorter the playing field, the easier the shot, so for an amateur playing at home, 4 feet by 8 feet is a good size for a table. The smaller table also is easier to fit into a small room, which may be the only area available at home. The angles are a little bit different on the smaller table, but as long as you have a cue stick in your hand to hit the cue ball, you can have a good time.

If you get a table much smaller than 4 feet by 8 feet, you're not going to have as much fun. It would be like playing with a toy. Also, small tables (bar tables) have a bigger cue ball, which is harder to control.

## Size of Pockets

The size of pool-table pockets varies. But keep in mind that the average pool ball is 2¼ inches in diameter, and you want to be able to pocket the ball with relative ease. If the pocket is the size of only two balls, the pocket is very tight and too formidable for the average player. When I had a table in my basement with 4½-inch pockets, nobody wanted to play me because it was so hard to pocket a ball.

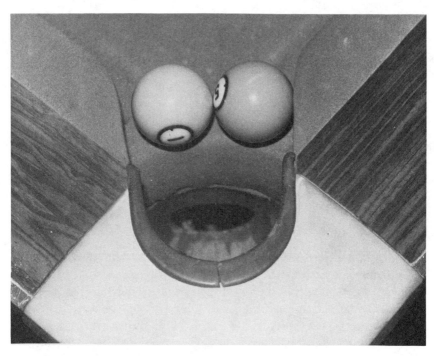

Wider pockets make for a more enjoyable game. This five-inch pocket can accommodate two billiard balls (each 2¼ inches in diameter).

This 4½-inch pocket is very tight for standard 2¼-inch billiard balls.

Most average players would feel the same way. They'd get frustrated and discouraged. If it takes you an hour and a half to sink 15 balls, you're going to say, "the heck with it" and take up another game. But if you sink four balls on the break and then make three in a row right after that, you're going to say, "Hey, this is a great game." It's nice, even in a commercial establishment, to have big pockets so people can have fun making their balls easily. The bigger the pocket, the easier it is to play.

To determine the size of a pocket, measure it from point to point, cushion to cushion, outside where the rail ends. All pockets on a given table should be the same size.

## Table Covering

If you want a cloth that covers the bed of your table to last a long time, get an all-wool cloth. If you're interested in the best playing surface with truer rolling speed that will last a fairly long time, get a nylon and wool blend. The greater the nylon content, the faster the roll; the more wool, the slower.

When cloth begins to wear out, the speed of the balls may be affected, so you should expect to recover your table every year or so. Incidentally, a worn cloth may indicate that an older table has a drift to one side or the other.

The cloth on modern tables comes in various colors. You should try to play on the same color all the time. So, even though gold is probably easiest on the eyes, you're probably wise to play on green-covered tables, since green is the most commonly found.

The best type of rubber to have on your table is True Speed, and most of the tables I've recommended come with it. If the one you buy or already own has a rubber you're not satisfied with, you can have it replaced.

## Lighting for the Table

The best table is of little value if you can't see what you're shooting at. So give it good light—fluorescent bulbs, if possible,

The light over your pocket billiards table should be centered so that there is an even distribution of illumination over the width and length of the table. An eight-foot fluorescent light is ideal.

or four 8-foot incandescent bulbs. Make sure the lighting is centered so the whole table is illuminated and there are no annoying shadows.

## Care of the Table

A pool table essentially takes care of itself, but you've got to clean it when it gets dirty, and you mustn't abuse it. Don't let the kids bowl on it or play Ping-Pong on it. Don't rap its sides with your cue stick, don't kick it, don't try to pick it up or walk around with it in some macho contest, and don't drop it. In short, don't do anything to your table that you wouldn't want done to you.

A table that's used extensively will get dirt on it, whether it's little pieces of chalk, dye from the chalk that comes off your hand, or just dust in the air.

You can clean the cloth with a brush, which really is the safe way, or with a vacuum cleaner, which is faster but dangerous. If you vacuum it, you have to be careful. Slate is in three parts held together by plaster of paris. If that plaster comes out, there will be two grooves the complete width of the table, over which the balls will have to travel. When brushing, do it toward the rack.

The rubber on a table, which is becoming standardized, doesn't need care because it's covered with cloth. But it is affected by humidity, so try to set up your table in a dry area.

The wood on the top rail of the table is usually covered by Formica or a comparable substance. To clean that, all you have to do is wipe it with a damp cloth. Polishing isn't necessary. It has a highly polished finish that should last a long time.

You might want to cover the table when you're not using it, to keep dust off.

## CUE STICKS

If you are serious about playing pool, you should have your own cue stick. This is so, even if all your playing is done in a billiard parlor, because you should always play with the same stick, one that's comfortable for you. It should improve your game by ten to fifteen percent.

Make sure the cue stick you buy is well made, properly balanced, and the right size. Try it out before you buy it.

What with that old devil inflation, be prepared to spend a minimum of $100 for a good cue. An average player might get a satisfactory cue for something under $100, but surely not under $50.

During World War II there was an expression, "Don't be fooled by the pretty face." Similarly, don't be fooled by how fancy a cue stick appears. *Fancy* and *good* are not synonymous in cue sticks. In fact, it may be the opposite, because anytime you start adding things to the stick to make it fancy, the structure is going to weaken. As in building a house, the more holes you put into it, the weaker it will be. Besides, pearls, diamonds, and ivories are not going to help you play.

The best cue sticks ever made were fashioned by the late George Balabushka of Brooklyn, New York. Like any work of art produced by someone who has since passed on, his cue sticks have now doubled in value. They just can't be duplicated.

Two of the best cue makers in the world today are Gus Szamboti of Philadelphia and Dick Helmsteader, who now lives in Japan. Gus specializes in custom cues; Dick is basically in the commercial cue line. I represent Adams Custom Cues, a company Dick founded, and I use a cue made by Dick, who does work for such top-notch players as Allen Hopkins and Jim Rempe.

Among other manufacturers of good cues are Danny James of Josh Cues East and Bill Stroud of Josh Cues West.

As good as these and some others are, as excellent as their equipment may be, they can't duplicate the touch and feel of my Balabushka. No one makes violins like Stradivari did!

## I "Wooden" Use Aluminum

Buy a wooden, rather than an aluminum, cue stick because temperature changes affect the feel of a metal cue more than they do the feel of the wooden one. Also, a wooden stick won't bend in half if you hit the table with it. It might chip, but not bend. The shaft of a good cue will be made of maple or another hardwood, and the butt will be of ebony or something like it. The wood should be as hard and dry as you can find. Moisture gets into the wood so it should be dried and cured before it's used.

## Two-Piece Is Better

Cue sticks are available in one- and two-piece models. I recommend the two-piece for the very simple reason that it is easier to carry. In the two-piece a metal screw at the top of the butt fits into the bottom of the shaft. Make sure that the parts of your cue stick fit together properly and the screw isn't off center. The one-piece has a couple of advantages: After it's seasoned, it won't warp or bend, and, unlike the two-piece, it

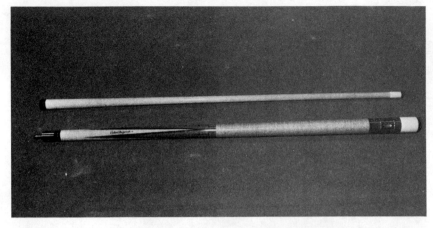

The parts of a cue stick should fit together perfectly, the butt screwing evenly into the threaded portion of the shaft. (My cue is shown in this photo.)

has no joint that might swell if it gets wet. But it's cumbersome to carry. So buy a two-piece.

When you are not using the cue, separate the butt and the shaft, and keep the parts in a case. A hard case has the advantage of giving better protection if it should be stepped on or run over. But more important is that it be lined with something to prevent moisture from seeping in. A fur lining is especially good, because of its smoothness. Fur won't cause any abrasion when the stick parts are being pulled out or put back into the case.

A fur-lined case offers the best protection against cold, heat, and other elements that could damage your cue stick. This is the inside of the one I use.

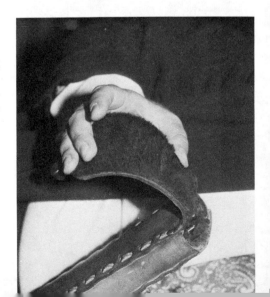

Putting your cue into the case properly is very important. If you don't place it properly you risk nicking your wrap and damaging the tips of your shafts. Put the butt in first, straight, then the shaft (or shafts). Never take the butt out of the case before the shafts, and when you remove the butt, pull it out straight, not on an angle. Otherwise, you may scratch the wrap, the wood, and anything else on the cue.

Dampness is a cue stick's natural enemy, so don't leave it where there is a lot of moisture. A place like the trunk of a car is also bad because of the sharp contrast in temperatures between night and day.

Don't lean the cue up against the wall and leave it there for a week, because naturally it is going to bend. When you are through using your cue, just unscrew it and put it back into the case.

Currently, the best case maker is Bob Hemple of Fellini Custom Cue Cases, a Texas firm. His cases are high-priced—$70 and up—but they are well worth the price, since they are well constructed and made out of animal skins. They do a fine job.

## Dimensions

A standard cue stick is 57 inches long, but most professional players use cues that are 58 inches in length, and I recommend you do the same. You'd be surprised what that extra inch can do. It will give you that much more reach on the table and often do away with the need to use the mechanical bridge (more about that later), a piece of equipment that is more of a hindrance than a help, in my opinion.

Even a child should not use a stick any shorter than the standard 57 inches; I began using that size when I was still in knee pants.

The circumference of the shaft of a cue ranges from 9mm to 14mm. Especially if you are a beginner, you should use the 13mm, because it provides more hitting surface.

As far as the weight of the cue is concerned, I don't believe in telling anybody else how heavy the cue should be. The weight of the cues most pros use is between 20 and 21 ounces. I prefer 21¼. Some pros recommend that you start with a light cue and work up to a heavier one, but I think that if you can handle it comfortably you should start with a fairly heavy one, 19½ ounces or more.

My advice about the dimensions of your cue applies, whatever your height, weight, reach, or physical proportions.

You should own just one cue stick. Using more than one will

affect your consistency adversely and sometimes give you an unfounded excuse for playing badly.

One time I was playing in a match in Elizabeth, New Jersey, with a backup cue stick because my Balabushka stick was in the shop being repaired. I lost so badly that I sneaked into a back office and deliberately broke the backup cue because I didn't want to use it anymore and go through the agony it entailed.

Next day, I used a different stick and played badly again. You can't blame it on the cue. But I should have had my Balabushka.

Usually, a cue stick can be repaired while you wait, but if it is something major that will require three or four days, you might be better off not playing.

You can use a spare cue, but it should be as close to your prime one as possible.

It's not a bad idea to carry an extra shaft for your two-piece cue stick in case the tip comes off the original shaft.

## The Tip

Be sure the leather tip of the cue stick is solid. It should be from about one-eighth to one-quarter of an inch high and have a good rounded shape, like a half-moon. It should have a nice crown to it.

A well-shaped cue tip is vital to playing well. Notice that the cue on the right has a tip that is shaped just right. It has a nice rounded crown; its sides are even with the white furl, and they're all blackened in. The tip at the left, however, extends over the edges of the furl. It's flat, not round, and it looks terrible. Don't play with a tip that looks this bad.

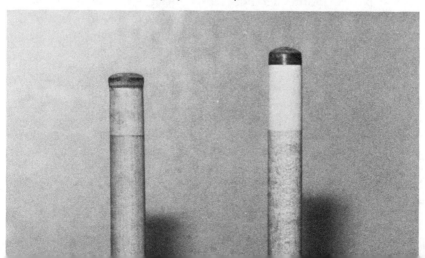

Avoid a soft tip because it will flatten out. My personal preference and that of most professional players is for a very hard tip, the harder the better. The one I like best is La Professional, made by a French company.

Obviously, the tip is an important part of the cue; if it should fall off, you can't really play. Tips, which usually come in quantities of 50, are a hit-and-miss affair. Sometimes you get a good one, sometimes a bad one.

### Cleaning the Tip

We like the edge of the tip to be round, dark, smooth, and shiny, so we rub it with a dollar bill. There is some kind of chemical agent in a dollar bill that has a nice effect on the leather tip. It would work with a five-dollar bill; in these inflationary times, a hundred-dollar bill works even better.

### White Furl

At the end of the shaft nearest the cue tip is white furl, usually made of ivory or buckhorn. Professionals avoid plastic. I wouldn't want anybody messing around with this part of the shaft, and neither should you because it can easily be nicked or scratched.

### The Wrap

One part of your cue stick that you have to watch very carefully is the wrap. If that should get nicked, you're naturally going to be aware of it; the stick will feel very funny in your hands.

What the cue is wrapped with depends on your personal preference. It might be Irish linen, leather, or nylon. I use and recommend Irish linen, because it absorbs the sweat from my hands better than leather, rubber, or any other substance would.

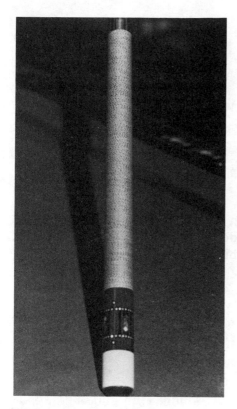

The wrap on the cue stick, the area where you grasp it, is usually strung tightly around the butt. Most professional players, myself included, prefer Irish linen. Be careful that someone doesn't try to sell you an imitation Irish linen. And make sure that none of the wrap is loose; once one strand comes apart, the rest will soon follow.

## Take Care

If you take care of it, a cue stick will last a long time. Here are some tips about taking care of it.

First of all, never use sandpaper on the cue stick, because you'll eventually get what we call "the pencil effect"—a point on your shaft. You start out with a shaft that is 13mm thick and very quickly get down to 11mm. Sometimes I don't follow my own advice and use an extremely fine grade of sandpaper—600A—but you shouldn't even use that.

The use of sandpaper will eventually wear the material away, and the stick is not going to be the same thickness or length as

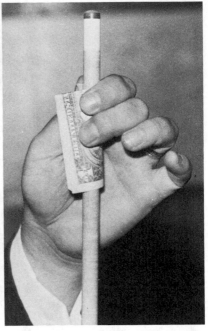

Never use sandpaper on the shaft. Even the finest grade will wear down the shaft until you don't have the right diameter, and eventually it's going to become a pencil.

I rub the shaft with a dollar bill, which takes off the dirt and gives the wood a kind of coating. The ink or chemical properties of the bill make the shaft smooth by closing the pores. Take a new, crisp bill and rub it into the shaft, and you'll see what I mean. To get off excess powder and possibly some of the excess dirt you can rub the cue with a clean towel. Whether you use a bill or a towel, rub fairly hard.

when you bought it. You selected the particular length and thickness because it felt right or it fit comfortably into your hand. But if you keep using sandpaper, you're going to wear it down, and you won't have the dimensions you wanted.

A trick a lot of players are using now is to rub the shaft with a dollar bill to create a nice shiny, filmy substance that takes all the dirt off and leaves an attractive finish.

A shaft really isn't true (it doesn't feel right) until it is seasoned with the oils, dirt, powder, and everything else from your hand. When it is, you will be aware of a big difference in the feel.

After you use a new shaft for a couple of weeks you ought to follow a procedure I've used with good results. I wet the shaft with fairly warm water on a washcloth. After it dries the pores are open, so I rub the shaft with lighter fluid on a towel or rag. This creates a sort of bonding or sealing effect on the shaft, filling the pores with an oily substance that makes the surface even and smooth.

Some people like lemon wax or lemon oil, but I find lighter fluid is a lot more effective, and I recommend it for anyone with a cue stick worth keeping in good shape. If the cue is valuable and it should get nicked, take it back to the person who made it and let him get the nick out.

## BALLS

The best balls, in the opinion of most championship players, are Brunswick Centennials, made by the Albany Billiard Ball Co. They used to cost about $30; now the price is around $100.

They seem to roll and react truer than other brands, though I suspect the difference in balls is often in the player's head. In a recent world tournament, for instance, the balls weren't opening on break shots, and we thought they were lighter than the Centennials. But we were assured the weight was identical.

Taking care of balls is simple. Use a cleaner to take dirt off and then a polisher. If you own a billiard room, I'd recommend that you buy a ball-polishing machine. It will save you a lot of time, energy, and effort. To keep the balls you have at home in good shape, just wash them occasionally with soap and water and then apply a little plastic polish.

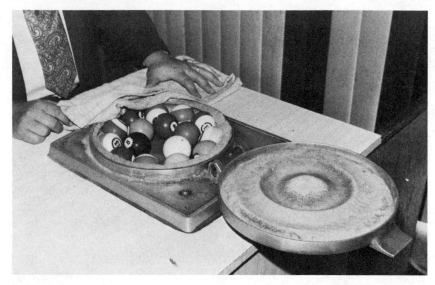

To keep your billiard balls clean, use a good billiard ball cleaner, some good polish, and a clean towel in conjunction with a billiard ball machine. When the balls come out of the ball machine, wipe them with the towel to take off the lint that adhered to them from the pads inside the machine. And remember, your billiard balls can't be clean if your ball machine is dirty.

## MECHANICAL BRIDGE

Years ago, the notched ends of most mechanical bridges were made out of metal, which caused a lot of difficulty. Any abrasion on the metal would prevent you from getting a smooth stroke and would badly scratch your cue.

Now bridges are made out of plastic, and this is a big advance. A man named Joe Russo in Trenton, New Jersey, makes what is probably the best bridge today: the Russo Interlocking Bridge. As the name suggests, his bridges neatly interlock. You can put two or three or even four together—just stack them up—and shoot over a mountain.

I know from experience how tough it is to use several mechanical bridges that don't interlock. If even one topples and you hit a ball other than the one you called, you lose your shot. So I advise you to get a few of the interlocking kind.

## TRIANGLE

Wood is the best material for a triangle for racking up balls. Plastic bends and breaks too easily.

Always use a wooden triangle for racking up balls.

## CHALK

Faulty chalk can cost you a match. It might make you miscue in a critical situation, costing you your turn, and then your opponent might go on to win the game.

It is important to have the right chalk. I'd go out of my way to get Masters, the best chalk made in recent years. It seldom cakes, it doesn't fall apart in your hand, and it seems to adhere to the tip better than any other chalk. Another good one is

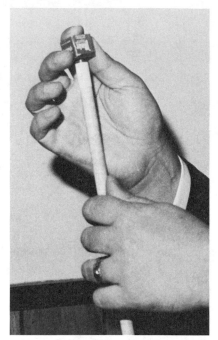

Chalk the tip of your cue stick by holding the chalk cube steady and rolling the stick between your palms and fingertips.

called National Tournament, made by Gandy, but I think Masters is best.

Chalk the tip of your cue stick before every shot or two. Don't apply the chalk by holding the stick and turning the chalk as if you were squeezing an orange. Instead, hold the chalk cube steady and rotate the stick in it by rolling it between your palms and fingertips. This way you should get an even distribution of chalk all around the tip. Examine it to make sure. If a spot was missed, fill in the missed areas with the edge of the chalk cube.

Always use a fairly new piece of chalk—rather than one with a deep hole in it—to avoid getting any chalk on the ivory or furl.

Don't leave your chalk in a damp place, because it will absorb moisture and, no matter what the brand, it will cake. Some jokers, fooling around, have tried to sabotage a player by wetting his chalk.

If the tip is so smooth that it won't take chalk, you can rough up the tip slightly with a file. Don't use the file in a scraping motion, or you will tear the tip. Just roll the tip lightly on the file, then wet the sides of the tip with a damp cloth and polish it, with either the back of sandpaper or a smooth piece of leather. This hardens the side and keeps the tip from extending beyond the sides.

## POWDER

If you're like me and have hands that sweat a lot, you should use powder on them. I've learned from experience, though, that

Don't powder your hands as if you were soothing a baby with diaper rash. You'll get the powder all over your suit and the table, and you'll be putting extra oil on your hand, making your cue stick very oily.

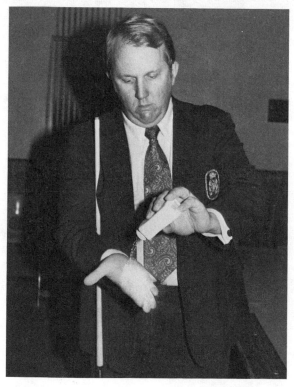

Just apply the powder on the parts of your hand
where the cue slides and use it sparingly. The
more powder you use, the more oily you'll get.

a lot of powders have a very oily base and leave an oily film on
your shaft that can play havoc with your game and mess up
your table. So look for a powder that doesn't have a particularly
oily base.

When you apply powder, use only a thin coat.

So much for equipment. Now some tips about the fundamentals of playing the game.

# 2

# Tips on Techniques

## STANCE

The best stance is the one that's comfortable for you. If you're not comfortable, you're probably in an awkward position, and that means you're going to be off balance and unable to hit the ball where and how you want it. Still, there are some guidelines you might want to follow:

You should place your feet so you won't be knocked over by a strong wind. Your feet should be spread slightly with your weight divided evenly between them. It's usually a good idea to bend your front knee slightly and keep your back knee straight, but certain shots will require an adjustment.

Your body should be closer to the table than the butt of your cue stick is. Your shooting arm (the right one if you're right-handed) should be able to swing freely, without interference from your body.

Don't stand up so straight that you can't get a good line of sight on the ball. But don't bend over so far that your body is

Here, I'm exaggerating to demonstrate a terrible stance. Notice how my feet are going in opposite directions, I'm standing bowlegged, and my chin is up in the air.

A good stance for stroking has the feet roughly parallel, a comfortable distance apart. One knee is slightly relaxed while the other is straight. The player's head is down over the cue.

too close to the cue stick and you are unable to swing your arm freely.

Players have different preferences about how close to keep the head over the cue. I'd suggest your head be about eight inches from the butt, over the cue, in the line of aim.

Your bridge hand should be about six to eight inches from the cue ball and your stroking hand about ten to twelve inches from the butt end of the cue stick. One way to tell whether you're at a comfortable distance from the cue ball is to place the cue tip almost on the cue ball. Hold your left arm (if you're right-handed) straight and hold the butt end of the cue in your right hand at your right hip. Once you feel comfortable, bend your body forward, keeping your eye directly over the cue stick.

A good way to check that your stance gives you good balance and freedom of movement for proper stroking is to have someone poke you in the shoulder with his or her index finger. If you lose your balance, your stance needs to be corrected.

## GRIP

Try to be consistent in the way you hold the cue stick. Grip it the same way every time you stroke, whether you're planning a long shot, a short shot, a cut, a draw, or whatever. Once you establish consistency by doing it the same way all the time, you will get better results.

You should grasp the butt about 10 to 12 inches from the end, which is about 4 inches behind the cue's balance point (where the weight of the cue is equal to the front and to the back).

Cradle the butt in the palm of your power hand, gripping it firmly with your thumb, index finger, and middle finger. The other two fingers come along just for the ride.

Don't leave any space between the cue and the skin between your thumb and index finger. Though you should hold the butt of the cue firmly, don't choke it. That's no way to treat a friend. The tighter you grip it, the worse you'll play, because you're putting so much tension on your arm. That tension is hard to control and you can't predict what will happen. Some players have a *slip stroke* in which they start at the top of the wrap as they practice-stroke and then slide their power hand back 12 inches to the bottom of the wrap for the actual stroke. This isn't possible if they're choking the cue.

So hold it tightly enough to control it, but keep it comfortable and don't choke it.

Here I'm grasping the butt of the cue stick much too tightly. All my fingers are on the cue as if I were choking a horse.

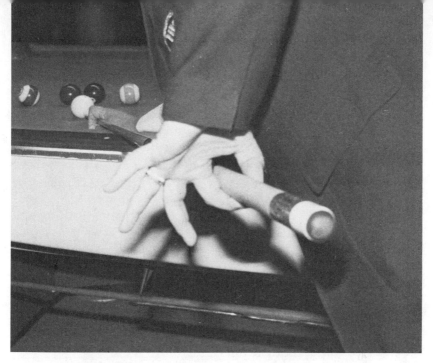

Here I'm grasping the butt too loosely. That space between the stick and my hand shouldn't be there.

This is the way you should hold the butt of the cue when you stroke—neither too tightly nor too loosely. Note that the butt is gripped by three of my fingers, and there is no space between the cue and my hand.

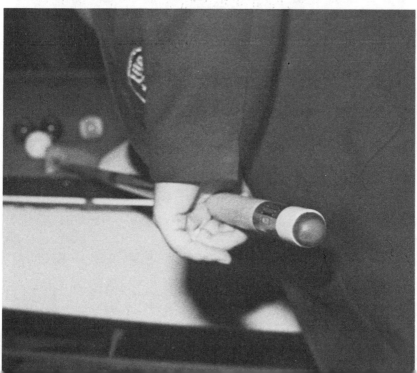

## STROKING

In stroking, your arm should move only from the elbow down. If you move your elbow or shoulder, your stroke will be uneven.

Your lower arm should swing like the pendulum of a grand-father clock, back and forth in a straight plane. Lifting the elbow will raise the cue, something you don't want to have happen.

How successful your stroke is depends largely on the wrist action of the power hand. Your wrist should act in coordination with your lower arm. As you swing your arm forward, your wrist should whip the cue stick into solid contact with the cue ball. Keep your wrist relatively loose; a flexible wrist gives better stroking action than a tight one.

A good stroke has a spring action that comes from the flowing together of wrist, elbow, and shoulder. If you're bringing your shoulder back and your arm forward, you're not going to get your body weight into it. If your wrist is not cocked and ready to spring, you won't get proper wrist action into the stroke.

With my elbow, shoulder, and wrist coordinated, I can make a ball go around the table three or four times very easily with a flick of the wrist and arm, while another player might not be able to accomplish that using his whole body. It isn't necessary to put your whole body into your swing. Your size doesn't have any bearing on the solidity of your stroke.

### Before and After

There are actions you should take before and after the stroke itself to get the best results.

To establish a groove for your swing, always take practice strokes before a shot. Always take the same number of practice strokes. Too many will make you tired; too few won't give you enough concentration to sight the ball properly. Professional players usually can get away with just going up there and stroking away, but amateurs can't. And even very good players

The way to shoot is to keep the butt of the cue stick as level as possible.

Try not to raise the butt of your cue the way I'm demonstrating here.

When you stroke the cue ball into the object ball it's important to have proper follow-through.

sometimes miss the easiest shots, usually because they rush into shooting.

I blew a shot in a tournament that could have meant thousands of dollars because I hit it without some warm-up strokes. Luckily, the shot put my opponent behind a cluster of balls that left him without a clear shot.

You can be sure that in my next turn I took all the time in the world and then took several warm-up strokes before taking, and making, the shot.

Before the stroke you need proper backswing. Bring your cue stick back a distance equal to the distance between your bridge hand and the cue ball, then hit a sharp, level shot.

After you stroke, make sure you follow through so that your cue tip winds up in front of the point at which the cue ball was located. To stroke the ball so it rolls true, follow through straight. Don't let the stick go off to the right or left.

Stay down in position and keep your cue stick on the table as long as reasonably possible after the shot. Keep your bridge hand in position, too, or you're likely to twist the cue stick and

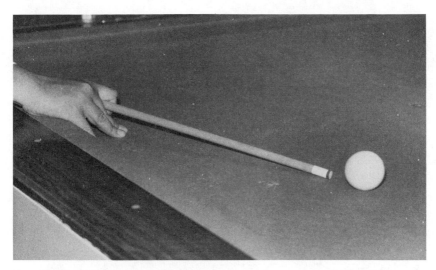

Your head should stay down, and so should your cue stick, with the cue ending at some point past where it contacted the cue ball.

Standing up with your head off the ball and the cue stick winding up in the air, as shown here, is improper follow-through.

spoil the shot. You should finish your stroke with the cue tip a few inches past where the cue ball rested. Don't let your cue tip waver around in the air after you stroke.

## Stroking Exercise

A good practice exercise for stroking is to place the cue ball about 18 inches from the head of the table and in a direct line with the middle diamonds at the foot and head of the table. Aim at the middle diamond at the foot of the table and try to make the ball come back along the same line so that it hits the end of the cue, which you left in follow-through position. You can do this only if you strike the ball exactly through the ball's center.

## SIGHTING

When you aim, your eyes look back and forth between the object ball and the cue ball. The last thing I sight is the object ball, to see if it goes in.

Most of the time you should hit the cue ball in the center. That way there is less chance of the cue tip slipping off. Also, a ball struck in the center rolls truer.

When you aim, mentally calculate the angle at which the cue ball will have to hit the object ball to drive it into the pocket. Then aim for the point you want to contact.

One way is to imagine a line drawn from the middle of the pocket through the center of the object ball. Then picture where on the back of that ball the imaginary line would come through and direct the cue ball to that point.

## HIT WITH AUTHORITY

You should hit every shot with speed and solidity. If you baby a ball, your cue stick will probably swivel. So hit with authority, but not so hard that you lose control.

The speed of your stroke should be uniform throughout the game, no matter what kind of shot you're making. The intensity of your stroke will depend on the situation. You'll use a much more gentle shot to make the cue ball hit only one cushion than you would to make it carom off nine. Use a short stroke if you don't want the ball to travel too far.

## BRIDGES

### Open versus Closed

Pick the bridge you find most comfortable, depending on such factors as how close the cue ball is to the rail and whether or not you have to go over another ball to hit the cue ball.

When possible, use a closed bridge, because this keeps the cue stick from flying up in the air or going somewhere you don't want it to. With an open bridge there's the danger of losing control, especially if you don't keep your head steady as you follow through.

When the cue ball is on the rail you might want to use an open bridge. It's good for a follow shot, too, while the closed bridge is better for a draw shot. In most ordinary situations on the table either type is good. To be safe, however, use the closed bridge, especially when you have to hit the ball hard.

A good distance for your bridge hand to be from the cue ball is six to eight inches, but this will vary with circumstances. If your bridge is too long, your cue tip will sway.

### Making a Bridge

A good way to make a bridge is to put your fist on the table with the knuckles resting on the bed. For an open bridge, you then lift your thumb to form the crevice where the cue stick will rest.

As an advanced player, you might want to try the flat open bridge. From the fist you made, open your fingers, keep your palm on the table, and raise your fingers slightly so that your hand bends. Elevate your thumb and cradle the cue between your thumb and index finger.

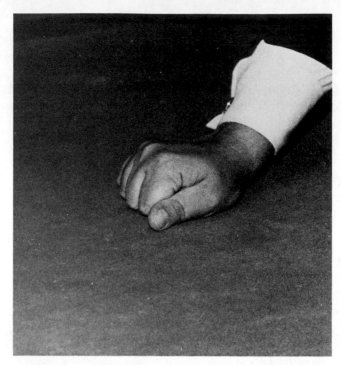

A good way to make your bridge is to place your nonpower hand (the right one if you're left-handed) on the table, knuckles down.

Extend the thumb of the fist you've made into the air.

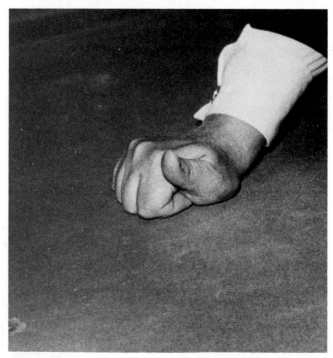

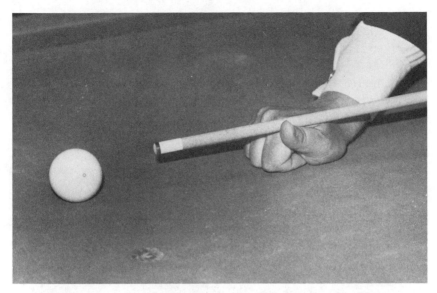

Let the cue stick glide between your upraised thumb and the side of the base knuckle of your index finger. This is a standard open bridge.

If you want to get more leverage for your open bridge, extend your fingers and press down on the pads of those fingers and the fleshy part of your palm below your thumb.

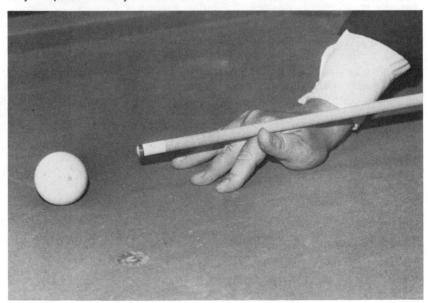

For a closed bridge, make a loop by raising your thumb and index finger and place their pads together. The cue stick will go through the loop. Spread out your other three fingers to give support. You might want to double under the second joint of your middle finger to strengthen that support.

If you're a little more advanced, you can make a closed bridge by putting your whole hand on the table with the heel of the hand firmly on the cloth. Then bend your index finger so the tip of it forms a loop against your thumb.

To make a closed bridge, go from the fist on the table to forming a loop by connecting the pads of your thumb and forefinger. The cue stick should be able to glide comfortably through that loop.

## Rail Bridges

When the cue ball is close to the rail, you should use a special bridge called a *rail bridge.*

If the cue ball is within about six inches of the rail, lay four fingers of your bridge hand across the rail and stroke through the middle and index finger, with your index finger over the cue and the thumb controlling it below.

If the cue ball is only an inch or two from the rail, use essentially the same bridge but pull your fingers back from the cushion. Loop your index finger around the cue with both your index finger and thumb off the rail, but the thumb braced against the outside of the rail. This gives greater control to the cue stick. Stroke through the loop of the index finger and alongside your middle finger.

If the cue ball is frozen against the rail, and the shot you're planning is about parallel to the rail, rest your thumb, index finger, and part of the heel of your hand on the rail, while the other fingers take a position on the bed.

Sometimes the cue ball is more than six inches from the rail but not far enough away to leave room for your whole bridge hand on the table. In this case, rest your bridge hand on the rail while your fingers and thumb hold the cue stick in the usual way.

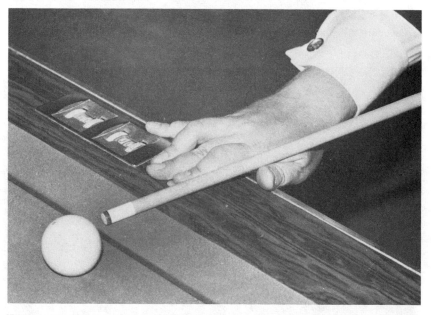

There are various types of bridges to use when the cue ball is near the rail and you want to use the rail for support. This is an open rail bridge usable when the cue ball is frozen to the rail. Note that the hand is off the table, as are part of the fingers.

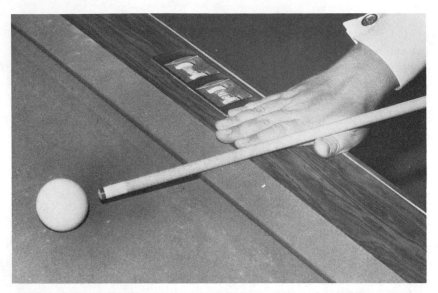

In this rail bridge the fingers are entirely on the rail and perfectly flat. This gives more security.

In this rail bridge the cue stick goes *under* the forefinger and glides along the rail.

I wouldn't recommend using this rail bridge, because your hand is in the air, and consequently it's going to be shaky and unsteady. Remember, you can move your hand, but not a table.

## Controlling the Bridge

Your bridge hand should control the shaft of the cue tightly enough so that the stick won't wobble, but loosely enough that it moves smoothly when you stroke.

In a closed bridge, don't leave an open space between the pads of your thumb and index finger because that doesn't leave a proper resting place for the cue. Don't let your index finger overlap your thumb because the cue will be too unsteady.

If the forward motion of the cue is held back by the skin of your index finger, you can tell you're holding the cue too tightly.

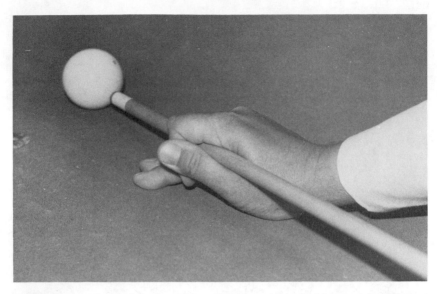

When the cue stick is gripped too tightly by your bridge hand as shown here, you won't be able to stroke smoothly.

Too much space between the cue stick and your forefinger is also something to avoid. When the cue stick is held too loosely you won't be able to control it properly.

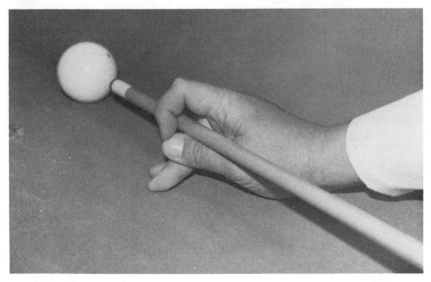

## Shooting Over a Ball

When you shoot over a ball, get your bridge hand as close as possible to that ball without touching the ball with your stick or hand. The closer you are to the ball, the more level your stroke. The stroke will be truer because you're not coming down on the ball.

Keep your fingers—from tips to first joints—on the table, pressing on them until you feel solid support. Don't stroke until you're sure the bridge is solid.

Raise the wrist and fingers of your bridge, not the butt of the cue. (To hit the cue ball low, lower your bridge, not the butt.)

When shooting over balls, be careful that your stick doesn't hit anything but the cue ball.

I know from experience what anguish that kind of accident can cause. I was defending my U.S. Open championship, which I had won for the first time a year before. I was playing Joe Balsis, who had me buried by about 109 to nothing. Then I got

In shooting over a ball, try to get your bridge hand as close as possible to the object ball you're shooting over (without touching it, of course). And try to keep your cue stick as level as possible.

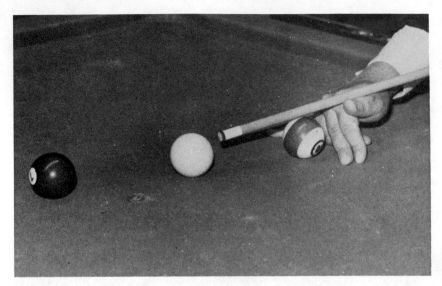

When the cue ball is a distance away from the object ball you're shooting over, the same principle applies. You'll find that in situations like this it's easier to keep your stick level.

up and started a run that brought me to within a hair's distance. I made a break shot, but the cue ball got stuck in the rack. A couple of balls came out, but all I could do was a very difficult shot in the upper corner. Because I was shooting over all the other balls, I had to make such a big bridge that my cue stick accidentally hit another ball, and the referee called a foul on me.

It was a controversial call, but it stood. Balsis got up and ran another 21 or 22 before he missed. I needed 45 to run out, and I ran them, for my second U.S. Open crown in a row. I've never forgotten how that accidental brush with my cue almost cost me the championship.

## Using the Mechanical Bridge

The best advice I can give you about the mechanical bridge is to try not to use it.

The "ladies' aid" or "crutch," as the mechanical bridge is

When you must use the mechanical bridge, be sure to keep it firm and flat on the table.

sometimes called, helps you make shots that are out of convenient arm's reach, but it's very difficult to control because it keeps you so far from the ball.

There are times, though, when you must use it, so here are some tips.

Lay the bridge on the table as flat as possible. Avoid the urge to lift the butt of the mechanical bridge. If you do lift it, the bridge will probably move at the notched end and result in a wobbly cue and an inaccurate shot.

To keep the bridge flat and steady, have your normal bridge hand hold it a few inches from the butt end between your middle and index fingers. Press down firmly on top of the butt of the bridge with the heel of that hand.

Keep the bridge on the side of the shot that's away from your

Don't do what a lot of players do—lift the butt of the mechanical bridge, as shown here.

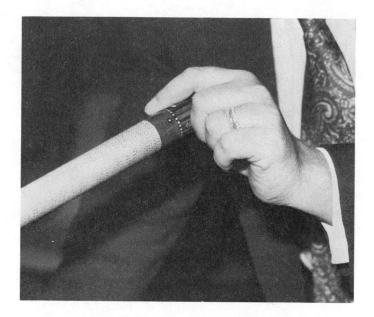

When you're stroking with the aid of a mechanical bridge, hold the butt of your cue stick this way (as shown above) not with palm underneath (as shown below).

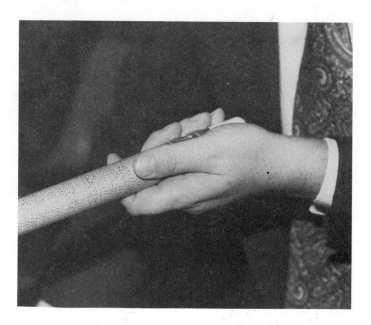

stroking hand. In other words, if you're right-handed, keep the bridge to the left of your shot.

Place the notched end of the bridge a few inches from the cue ball. Which notch you put the cue stick through depends on which spot on the cue ball you want to hit. Whether or not you place it so the high notched part is up depends on how the balls lie. If you want to shoot over a ball, the high part will be up.

Grip the butt of the cue with what is essentially a turned-up version of your usual grip. Place the cue on your thumb with your middle and index fingers on top of the stick, almost as if you were shooting a dart. Sight down the cue stick to the cue ball and then stroke as if you were throwing a dart with either an overhand or a sidearm motion. Your stroking action will come mostly from the wrist.

# 3
# Tips on Special Shots

## DRAW, FOLLOW, STICKING

Until you get really good at shooting pool your best bet is to aim to hit the cue ball dead center. Once you've mastered that, you can attempt the different types of shots that are required during a game.

When you want the cue ball to *follow* or move forward after it strikes the object ball, hit the cue ball above center. Keep your cue level and follow straight through. Don't hit the cue ball at the extreme top because you take too much of a risk of miscuing. It also spoils your accuracy and the desired action of the shot. Keep your bridge hand in a position that enables you to keep your cue level.

If you want to *draw* the cue ball back toward you after it makes contact with the object ball, hit the cue ball below center. Keep your cue level and follow straight through. The lower you strike the cue ball, the greater the amount of draw. How hard and fast you stroke will also affect how much draw results. Don't hit the ball at the extreme bottom because you'll cause it

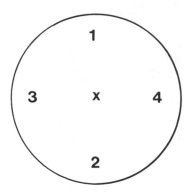

For follow, hit cue ball above center (#1). For draw, hit it below center (#2). To apply left-hand English, hit cue ball to left of center (#3). For right-hand English, hit it right of center (#4).

to jump. (Deliberate jumping means a point penalty and loss of turn in some competitions.)

Note that your follow-through should be straight, no matter what kind of stroke you hit.

I've emphasized the importance of elevating or lowering your bridge hand rather than the butt of your cue stick. However, there may be times when you have to elevate the butt of the cue to draw successfully—say, when the cue ball is near the rail or you have to stroke over an object ball. When raising the butt *is* necessary, make believe the "equator" of the ball is at the same angle as the one in which you're holding your cue. Then hit the cue ball below that axis.

Sometimes you'll want the cue ball to stop dead after it hits an object ball. This is known as *sticking*. To do it, just hit the cue ball a little below center, but not as low or as hard as you would to draw. Just how far below center you hit the cue ball depends on your distance from the object ball. The closer you are, the less distance you need to hit it below center. Hit the ball only at a normal rate of speed.

It is hard to make the cue ball stick on a new cloth, especially if it's nylon, because that tends to make the ball go farther.

## ENGLISH

English consists of hitting the cue ball to the right or left of center to make it spin one way and curve the other. It also causes the first object ball the cue ball strikes to spin in the direction opposite that of the cue ball.

You create right-hand English by striking the cue ball to the right of center, left-hand English by striking it left of center.

Right-hand English makes the cue ball spin counterclockwise, or left, while curving clockwise, or right. Left-hand English has just the opposite effect.

Use English as seldom as possible because you can get into more trouble applying it incorrectly than if not using it at all.

When you must use it, make your stroke sharp and springy and follow through. Remember to compensate—allow for the curved path a ball takes when English has been applied.

On about 99 percent of all shots you can apply the required

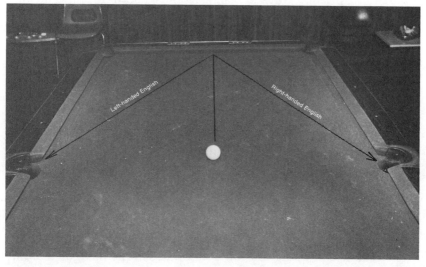

When left-handed English is applied the cue ball will spin clockwise but travel counterclockwise (left) after hitting the cushion. When right-hand English is applied the cue ball will spin counterclockwise but travel clockwise (right) after hitting the cushion.

English by striking the cue ball only a cue tip's width from the center. If you go wider than that, you take too much of a chance of miscuing or missing the shot.

## Natural and Reverse English

There are two basic kinds of English—natural and reverse.

It's natural (or running) English when you hit the cue ball on the same side as the direction you want it to travel after it hits the object ball or cushion. A cue ball hit to the left of center, for instance, will travel left after it hits the object ball or cushion.

It's reverse English when you apply it to the side of the cue ball that is *opposite* the direction you want it to travel after it hits an object ball or a cushion. The cue ball, in effect, reverses itself.

"High" English is achieved by simultaneously applying English and hitting the ball above center.

You have to keep in mind certain physical phenomena that happen with each. Natural English adds speed to the cue ball after it hits and widens the angle of the ball caroming off the cushion. Reverse English slows the speed of the ball, narrows the angle, and actually reverses the course the cue ball would normally travel after striking a cushion.

With natural English you have to take into account that the longer the shot, the wider the arc of the cue ball's curve will be. Say you have a table-length shot in which you want to just barely touch the object ball on its left side. A left-hand English shot might curve too much and miss the object ball. So what you should do is estimate the curve and compensate by aiming to hit more of the object ball.

Table and atmospheric conditions affect English. On a brand-new cloth or in dry weather a shot on which English is applied will be longer. In damp weather the same type of English applied to a ball going the same amount of rails has got to come up a little shorter. If you're playing in damp weather, you have to remember to be a bit quicker.

## BANKS, CAROMS, AND COMBINATIONS

If you're a beginner, it is difficult enough to make the ball go straight where and how you want it, so avoid the complications of a *carom, bank,* or *combination* shot as long as possible.

When you're ready to try them, there are some pointers to keep in mind.

### Caroms

One type of carom (or *kiss,* as it is sometimes called) is a shot in which you ricochet the cue ball off one object ball and into another, pocketing the second object ball. Or it might involve caroming one object ball off a second, with the first one proceeding to the pocket. Often you'll want a ball to glance off another for the sake of positioning, and that's fine. But when it happens by accident the balls can end up frozen, touching a rail or each other, in a way that is nothing but troublesome.

In this kiss shot I'll have the cue ball make the first object ball contact the second and proceed into the side pocket opposite me.

## Banks

A bank shot is one in which you drive the object ball into one or more cushions on its way to the pocket. Remember that in a bank shot the angle increases as the speed of the ball increases.

When banking a ball, estimate the space between the ball and the pocket nearest to it. Then mentally bisect the angle and try to drive the ball to a point that is halfway between the ball and the pocket.

In this bank shot I'll drive the object ball against the opposite cushion and have it come back into the side pocket near me.

## Combinations

A combination shot involves driving the cue ball into one or more object balls, which in turn strike the object ball you're trying to pocket.

It sounds dramatic, but avoid the temptation to try it, if at all possible. Unless the combination is lined up absolutely straight for the hole, take a different shot. If you have a straight-in shot

In this straightforward combination shot the cue ball will knock the nearest object ball into the second, which in turn will knock the third ball into the side pocket opposite me.

besides the combination possibility, by all means take the straight-in one first.

Sometimes, of course, there's no alternative but to take the combination. In that case, pay close attention to the ball just before the one you're trying to pocket. That's the key, because it will tell you whether the angle is proper for making the shot.

# 4
# Tips on Practicing

## LESSONS

If you want to start out playing pool the right way, take lessons from a pro, who can not only teach you the basics but also give you the know-how on which shots can be made and which cannot. It will probably cost you $20 to $100 an hour, but it's a worthwhile investment if you're serious about playing.

Ask the owner of a billiard room to suggest a capable teacher. Not every good player is a good instructor, but few players will undertake a teaching assignment if they're not capable of instructing you in the fundamentals and telling you what you're doing wrong.

## PRACTICE

The real learning begins after the lessons are over.

Any pro, myself included, can tell you how to play—how to

To get yourself off to a good start in pocket billiards, take lessons from a pro. Here I'm helping a novice make a proper closed bridge.

stroke, chalk up, make your bridge, and all the rest. But I can't make the ball go into the pocket for you. *You've* got to make the ball go into the pocket, and that's the whole game.

You learn to do it by practicing. To tell the truth, I'm not a big advocate of practice. I used to practice a lot, but now I find it boring, and you will, too, unless you make it meaningful for yourself. If you just go and hit a rack of balls by yourself, you're not going to gain much benefit. But if you practice with some purpose, it can not only be worthwhile but it might even be enjoyable, especially if you practice with someone.

Regular practice means daily practice. An hour a day ought to add up to meaningful time without boring you. Keep to that daily routine until you're good enough to get by with less practice.

Once you've mastered the fundamentals, you should practice with another person. It will give you a sense of competition, so you'll try harder. Also, your opponent will be able to point out your mistakes, some of which you might not have become aware of by yourself.

Playing a regular game of straight pool is probably the best thing to start with because it gives you experience in pocketing the ball, without being as difficult as some of the more complicated games.

What should you practice? Practice your touch, your feel, your timing, your sense of the game. You might know how much left-hand English to use, but you might not have the proper touch to do what you want; you might know how much draw to use, but you might draw three feet farther than you wanted to.

Practice shots you're weak in; they may become your strongest shots. When I was first learning to play I used to practice side shots. I'd put the cue ball down with some object balls all over the table and just cut them into the side pockets from all different angles. That's why I became such a good side-pocket shooter.

One type of shot everyone can profit from practicing is the long shot. Just hit the cue ball hard and concentrate only on making the ball at the end of the table. Forget about position when you're practicing long shots. Remember, as I noted earlier, your first objective when you're playing pool is to make the ball in the pocket. What's the sense of playing good position if you don't make the ball?

## Practice Exercises

Once you're making the ball in the pocket with regularity, try the drills I recommend for position play later in this chapter.

Actually, you don't even need a pool table to practice some aspects of the game. In school when I was a kid I'd pretend my pencil was the cue stick and practice making bridges. (I'd hide behind the kid in front of me so the teacher wouldn't see me.)

When I got to the pool room after school I would naturally practice on the pool table what I had practiced in school. You could do the same.

You could also take a broomstick and pretend it's a cue stick and just practice stroking. Or you could stand by your kitchen table, which is about the height of a pool table, and try out different stances until you determine what feels comfortable.

## WATCH AND IMITATE

Probably the most valuable tip I can offer anyone who wants to play like the masters is to watch and imitate.

If you get a chance, go to a professional pool tournament and watch the great players do their thing. Form a mental picture of how they make a bridge, how they stand next to the table, their whole general makeup. And then try to emulate those who capture your fancy. Copy your heroes.

You may see several players you admire whose styles are completely different. Try one style for a reasonable period of time and then, if that doesn't suit you, try the other. If, for example, I make a bridge with my finger one way and you try it and find it uncomfortable, check to see how someone like Allen Hopkins makes his bridge and try to do it his way. If that turns out to be comfortable for you, then that's the bridge-forming style you should use.

I learned by watching and imitating.

## POSITION

In pool, position basically means planning ahead, picking your next shot or shots, and then not only pocketing a ball but also having the cue ball get into position to pocket the next one.

If you're a beginning player, you shouldn't concern yourself too much with position. You have to learn how to put the ball into the pocket first. What good is knowing position if you can't make the shot? People will argue that it's no good making one shot if you're not in position for the next, but at least you make one shot. So first concentrate on making the ball; the rest will come later.

When I was first taught how to play I didn't know anything about position. My father kept telling me, "You've got to play position." Well, I kept trying, but I just couldn't do it. Then, when I was about 18, I suddenly started to play the right type of position.

Position isn't something you can learn; it's something you have to develop—by the touch, by the feel. Some tips about position follow.

Always take the shot you think you can make, and if you're a beginning player, take the easiest shot first.

When all 15 balls are on the table, look only one or two shots ahead. When you're down to a few balls—say, five—decide in what order you want to play them and try to position your cue ball on each shot accordingly.

Don't try position play on the break or when you're trying to scatter a cluster, because you can't predict what will happen. And when you break up a cluster, don't scatter the balls too

For best position play, pocket the balls in the order shown here, beginning with 1. The ball designated as the fifth one you hit would be the key ball (the one you pocket next to last). When you make that one the cue ball should not travel at all, and it would be in perfect line with the break ball, number 6.

hard. You want all the balls on the same half of the table.

Try to hit the smallest number of balls possible on one shot. Try to play into the four pockets that are at the middle and foot rails of the table, rather than in all six pockets, because you don't want to have to shoot your cue ball up and down the table.

Imagine a line through the middle spot bisecting the table crosswise and concentrate on working in the area from there to the foot of the table. Should any balls go up to the other end, try to pick them off as soon as possible.

When you're ready to practice position there are a couple of good practice drills I'd recommend.

In one, you place about a dozen balls in a circle in the middle of the table, with the cue ball inside the circle. You should try to pocket all the balls, one at a time, without letting the cue ball hit a rail. If you miss, you lose.  You'll need your whole repertoire of follow, draw, and English shots to pull this off.

A good position drill is to line up all the object balls in a circle with the cue ball in the middle, and then pocket the balls one at a time without having the cue ball touch a rail or another object ball.

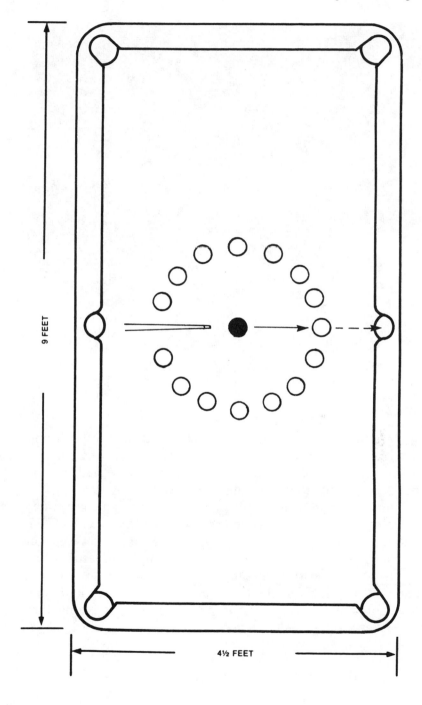

9 FEET

4½ FEET

Form the object balls into an L shape about two diamonds away from a corner pocket. Place the cue ball outside the L and then pocket each of the object balls in that corner pocket. Try to make your L straighter than I did here.

In the other drill, you place an object ball at the foot spot and create a large L with all the other balls. Then place the cue ball anywhere outside the L and try to pocket all the balls in the corner pocket, beginning with the ball closest to the rail.

As good as professional pool players are, we can't guarantee we're going to be in the exact spot we want for the next ball. We try, of course, to get as close as possible. If we don't get right on the money, we have to make do with what we have. Usually, we play into a circle with a six- to nine-inch diameter around the location of the ideal spot. The reason we are pros and play better than others is that most of the time we'll be within that circle. Other people won't.

# 5
# Tips on Competing

## NATURAL TALENT

Few people are born pool champions, but there is such a thing as natural talent, especially a gift for eye–hand coordination. I was a pretty good player when I was six years old. But that doesn't mean I haven't had to work at it ever since.

Whether or not you have so-called natural talent, you can still develop into a very good player. This is true regardless of your age, gender, size, build, or strength. But you have to be willing to work hard.

To play the game well, you have to be mentally and physically ready and have the coordination to achieve the shots.

The better your eyesight, the more finely you can cut a ball. That's not to say that poor eyesight eliminates your chances of being good at the game. (I happen to be nearsighted, but I don't have to wear glasses at the pool table.) If you have to wear glasses, you can still learn to play well. Compensate by concentrating on position play, so you won't have to cut the ball as precisely. If you leave yourself a shot that has a relatively easy angle, you won't have to do very much squinting and precision shooting to make the shot.

## MENTAL AND PHYSICAL PREPARATION

To get yourself mentally ready for a game, there are some things you should avoid. Don't have an argument with your sibling, spouse, or anyone else. Personal problems are going to interfere with your concentration, whether you're playing in a championship match in a auditorium or in a friendly game in your basement. So, as much as possible, leave your worries behind you and concentrate totally on the game. Block out that argument, the crowd, how good your opponent is, and give the game all you've got.

In order to win, you've got to believe you can. I went into the finals of the U.S. Open against Luther Lassiter, who was a very feared, knowledgeable competitor at the time. Even though I was very much the underdog, I had been riding a hot streak and I was confident that I could triumph.

The game opened with each of us taking a couple of scratches apiece. Then I made a shot and ran 107. I'd hoped to run 150 and out. Then, going for point number 108, I made the object ball, but the cue ball went up the table and down the table, in among all 14 balls, and scratched.

So Luther got up and started running the balls—42, 56, 70, 84. Now he had 87 and a break shot, a hanger. He called time and went to the bathroom. When he came back he missed the ball and busted the pack wide open. I ran the 40-plus I needed to win the game. It was the most thrilling thing that ever happened to me in pool and will be as long as I live. It was my first U.S. Open championship.

I was so scared and shaky that they had to get a chair for me. I had tears in my eyes for half an hour, I was so happy. It was the most exciting victory I've ever had.

The next year I beat Joe Balsis (as recounted earlier); then it came down to Luther Lassiter and me again in the third year. We both played badly—it was the most horrible championship series you'd ever want to see—but I won my third U.S. Open title in a row.

At the following Open I beat Danny DiLiberto for my fourth and last U.S. Open championship. After four years of winning I was beginning to let down some mentally.

Something that needs improvement in my own attitude is that I hardly concentrate in double-elimination tournaments when I come into the finals without having been defeated. If my opponent beats me and I have no losses, he's got to come back and beat me again. That's the way it was in the Open championship play. I was never really serious during the first game, because even if I lost that, I'd still have another in which I could win the championship.

## PRESSURE

If you're lucky, you'll be able to perform well under pressure. I seem to thrive on it, but that wasn't always the case.

In Elgin, Illinois, in 1966, in my first major tournament, Frank McGown, Irving Crane, and I were tied, so we had a three-man play-off to determine which two would be in the final match. Total points would decide which two would be the finalists.

I played Crane first, and he beat me. Then McGown lost to Crane, too. Now I was playing McGown, and I would have to beat him by something like 31 balls in order to get into the finals with Crane. I got within one point of what I needed, while Frank needed 13 points to get by me.

I was shooting, and I had a hanger, a shot so easy that anybody who can hold a cue stick could make it. The ball was four inches from the hole, and I couldn't wait to pocket it. I stroked the cue ball into the object ball, which hit the side cushion and then the bottom cushion, and just went back and forth from point to point, finally coming to rest in the jaw of the hole.

I was stretching across the table and, as I saw the ball jaw, I blacked out. I just put my head down, and my body came to rest. Luckily, I didn't move any balls in fainting.

What awakened me was someone yelling, "Cut!" A camera crew had been filming the match for television, and they now had to reload their equipment. As if I wasn't already crazy with tension, this added to it. I started walking around, yelling at myself, "How could I do this?" Now the camera had been reloaded, and it was McGown's turn to shoot. The cue ball, fortunately for me, had come off the rail and had him snookered. He tried to kick the object ball in off the side rail, but he missed it by a foot.

I eagerly grasped my cue stick, bent over the table, and was ready to put the hanger in the pocket once and for all. But, because I'd just missed a shot as a result of rushing it, I made sure I took enough time now. I stood up and went back to the player's chair, chalked up and powdered up. I got back down on the table, but stopped again, walked back to the chair, took a drink of soda just to cool down and calm my nerves. I put a little more chalk on my cue tip to make sure I didn't miscue. Then I went back and sank the ball.

But the tension wasn't gone; I had to go right into the finals against Crane, who'd been calmly sitting by, enjoying the comedy of errors.

I tried to calm myself but couldn't. And, as I said earlier, I lost to Crane, even though I could have beaten him.

Other times, I've done some of my best pool shooting under pressure. If I had to make a shot, I made it—no matter what was at stake. Don't be upset if you're not able to withstand pressure. If you can't make the big shot when the chips are down, accept that fact and keep plugging.

## HABITS THAT RELAX

Try to be aware of habits that tend to relax you, such as powdering your hands before a match or rubbing your cue stick with a dollar bill. If there are superstitious habits that relax you, stay with them. Some players wear favorite clothes when they compete (such as white socks, even with a tuxedo); one player used to whistle constantly.

Some players relax before a match by sleeping or reading or watching TV. Others won't watch the tube or read a paper, not for reasons of superstition but because they don't want to do anything to hurt their eyes. You might want to rest your eyes by keeping them closed for half an hour before a match.

In general, you play best when you're in the best of health, so try to avoid playing with a cold or other illness and get as much rest as possible. Alcohol will hurt your game, so don't drink. And stay out of smoke-filled rooms, where your eyes are likely to become irritated.

Try to keep your weight down. Thinner players seem to have more endurance than their chubbier competitors.

Pros disagree about whether or not it's okay to eat a short time before a meal. Irving Crane can't play until at least two or three hours after eating. Others can play just after they've eaten without any ill effects. I can't play on an empty stomach, but too much food too close to game time will bother me. You'll find out for yourself what you can handle.

You should dress as comfortably as the rules allow. Loose-fitting clothing is best because it doesn't interfere with the fluid motion of your stroke.

## WALK AWAY

As important as it is to leave your problems at home, it's equally essential that you let nothing distract you in the billiard room. If someone at another table makes a super shot just as you're going to stroke, do the commonsense thing and walk away from the table. Take a drink of water or perform some other time-killing ritual to keep you calm and wait until the hubbub dies down before taking your shot.

Once, when I was 17 and needed just one more ball for an upset victory in a U.S. Open tournament, the crowd was excited. So I put my cue stick down and walked around the auditorium, gesturing for quiet. When the crowd did settle down I took my shot and made it. Not everyone can be that cool. A friend of mine gets so nervous when he plays that he constantly jumps and dances around. Once he spun around and accidentally hit the referee with his cue stick, knocking him out.

Because pool is a game that can be won or lost by a fraction of an inch, it's important not to let anything disturb you. That's not always easy. Some players will do just about anything to throw their opponent's game off. One fellow I was playing went to the bathroom seven times during one rack of balls! Luther Lassiter, known as "Wimpy" because of his fondness for hamburgers, used to eat them during a match but denied it was to psych out an opponent. Sometimes a player's friend or relative will casually wave a handkerchief when his opponent is about to shoot, hoping he'll watch the hanky instead of his game.

## SELF-CONFIDENCE, NOT OVERCONFIDENCE

You've got to believe you can succeed at the game, and wanting to do it is the first step.

But guard against overconfidence, which can cost you points and games. Pool is an easy game to handicap. You can spot points, games, anything to even up a match. There's no formula I can give you as to how much of a handicap you can give safely. Just be sure to base it on real differences between you and don't go wild. In a short game, it's possible for anyone to beat anyone else unless they're in completely different classes.

An exaggerated opinion of yourself might lead you to spot an opponent 49 points in a 50-point game, ignoring the simple fact that he or she needs just one point to win. You might think a shot is so easy that you won't take practice strokes, and you'll blow the shot. Or you may think you can make any shot on the table, so you shoot wildly.

## TAKE RISKS

At the same time, without going wild, you've got to be willing to take risks occasionally in order to win. (This is my theory because I'm an offensive player! Other top players may tend to disagree.) If you do take a risk, stay sufficiently cool and take enough time to give yourself the best chance of making the ball.

If there's a trouble ball that should be pocketed right away lest your opponent start a game-winning run, then go for it, even if it involves a bit of a gamble.

You can divide good players into two main categories— offensive and defensive. I'm an offensive player, a shot maker who would rather try to pocket a ball even on a tough shot than play safe. Joe Balsis is a very powerful player along the same lines. When I was first coming up, he was the player I was most afraid of. Joe is a muscle player who doesn't baby the ball but hits it with authority and puts it into the hole most of the time.

When someone is playing well you can hear the ball going into the hole—*whap, whap, whap!* The sound is so devastating that it inspires fear in the player's opponents.

Whether you should play that way is determined by your individual style. If you want to run 70 and play safe, that's fine. If you want to run 70 and take a chance on running 140, that's fine, too. Irving Crane is not a shot maker; he'd rather play safe than go for a tough shot. He doesn't take chances; I do.

If you don't think you can make a particularly tough shot, don't try it. You have to believe you can make any shot you attempt. I'm convinced that any shot I call I can make; I don't shoot saying, "This can't go." Certainly, there are situations in which your confidence wavers about making the shot as you're looking it over. If I thought a shot probably couldn't go but had a chance, I might shoot it, while Crane never would in the same situation.

In any event, don't let up. Play as hard as you can, no matter what the competition seems to be, until the last ball is pocketed. I once played some youngsters I was so sure I could beat that I took it easy on them. I wanted them to get some time at the table. Two of them had *too much* time at the table—they beat me.

If you're way ahead of someone, you might be tempted to let up in order to spare your opponent humiliation. But the tide can turn so easily; your opponent could run out, and the humiliation would be yours.

## GETTING BETTER

Always believe you're going to get better. You will.

There's always room for improvement, even for the pros. I don't believe I've mastered pool yet. When my father was teaching me how to play years ago, there were certain things he could do at the table that I could not. Now there are things I'm able to do that he isn't. He still has room to learn, and so do I.

Recently I met a 75-year-old man who's been playing pool for 55 years and is still at the game. He hasn't given up. His physical condition may hamper him, maybe his eyesight is going, but he still hasn't given up. No matter how old you are or how long you've been playing the game, there's still room for improvement.

## FOUL!

In a straight pool tournament, if you move a ball with your hand or anything else, it's usually a foul, and you lose your turn. In Chicago, I once put my hand on the table, the cloth of which was a little loose. As I tried to steady my bridge, the cloth moved, and so did the ball. I never touched the ball, but the referee called a foul. I wanted to protest but decided there was no point.

In a more recent year in Connecticut I was playing a nine-ball match against Jack Colavita, a fellow from New Jersey, and I had him buried. I shot from behind the stack, and the cue ball came off the rail, hit the ball it was supposed to hit, and then caromed off the 8-ball and pocketed the 9-ball. The referee, thinking I had hit the wrong ball nearby, called a foul. It was obvious to everybody else in the place that I hadn't fouled; and I said, "What? How could you call that a foul?" But his decision stood.

As upset as you may be about a bad call, you can't do more than maybe mutter something like "blind bat" at the referee and sit down. After all, you're playing in front of hundreds of spectators. In addition, if you were to verbally abuse him, he might hold a grudge and do the same thing again.

There are times when, if we have a disagreement with a referee we'll tell the tournament director that we want the ref removed because he's making bad calls. But we try not to. A referee in pool is like an official in basketball, tennis, hockey, or any other sport. His call will stand unless it's such a flagrant mistake that the official on hand—in this case, the tournament director—reverses the decision. But I've seldom seen that happen.

You'd be smart to guard against letting a bad call blow your cool or using the call or the ref as a scapegoat for your bad play.

# 6

# Games

Of the innumerable fun-filled games that can be played on a pool table, four rate as the most popular wherever pocket billiards is played. Let's take a look at these established old favorites, along with one new game that looks like a winner, and see how you can best apply to them the skills you've learned.

## 14:1 CONTINUOUS POCKET BILLIARDS

If you can play a good game of 14:1 Continuous Pocket Billiards, also known as Straight Pool or Call Shot, you can play any pool game well.

The object of 14:1 is to score a preset number of points before your opponent does. The winning score is usually 50 or 100 points; in championship play, 150.

As you know, you have to call the object ball you're planning to sink, as well as the pocket you're aiming for. You get a point for every called object ball you hit into a designated pocket and for any that go into the pocket along with the ball that was called.

Take a few practice shots before you begin a game on an unfamiliar table.

To start the game of 14:1, all 15 object balls are racked up in the triangle at the foot spot. The player who starts has the cue ball in hand—that is, he or she can place the ball anywhere between the head string and the head of the table.

To decide who breaks, players generally *lag,* that is, hit a ball from behind the head string so that it contacts the foot rail and returns. The player whose ball lands closer to the head rail has the choice of whether he or his opponent breaks.

*Tip:* If you win the lag, choose *not* to break. The chance of making a called shot on the break is too slim, and it's very likely that you'll set up an easy shot for your opponent.

For the opening break I put the cue ball to the right of center about 1½ diamonds over along the head string.

If it's you who must break, try to hit the cue ball in such a way that you leave your opponent with either no shot or with a tough one. The player who breaks usually doesn't call a ball and pocket because chances are so thin of his being successful. But you have nothing to lose to call a ball and pocket, should it go in on a fluke. If a ball that wasn't called does go into a pocket, it's spotted at the foot string and there is no score.

To break, set your cue ball along the head string at the side you find more comfortable. I put it to the right and, using right-hand English, I try to clip just about a quarter of the ball that's in the rear right-hand corner of the triangle.

Remember, the rules require you to drive two or more of the object balls, in addition to the cue ball, to a cushion or put an object ball into a pocket. If you scratch the cue ball into the pocket without hitting two balls into the rail, you lose *two* points. (That's another good reason you should have your opponent break.)

I try to have the cue ball hit about a quarter of the ball in the right rear corner of the rack.

The two balls in the rear corners of the rack move a little from the other balls, while the cue ball hits the rear cushion and comes back up the table, leaving my opponent with nothing good to shoot at.

I hit the cue ball to the right of center to give it right-hand English and have it bounce off the rear cushion at one of the diamonds, hit a side rail at a diamond near the foot of the table, and then hit a diamond on the opposite side of the table.

After the break, when it's your turn, if you have a choice of hitting a close shot or a distant one, take the one that's nearer. It's almost always the easier shot. A more advanced player might take the more distant, for reasons of position, but it's better to be safe. Don't call a ball unless you're reasonably sure you can pocket it.

When the balls are spread out from one end of the table to the other, clear the head of the table first (if you can), then work your way down to the rack area.

Try to avoid having your cue ball graze any ball besides the

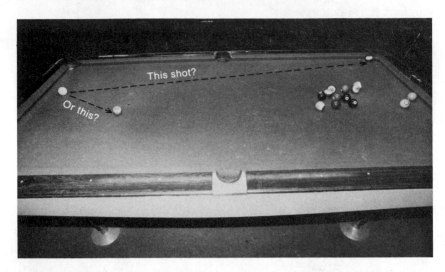

Always take the shot at the ball you can make. In this situation you have the choice of trying to make the nearest ball in the side pocket or the farthest ball in the corner pocket. Which one should you aim for? The one at the foot of the table, because it's so close to the pocket.

That cluster of three balls near the side rail spells trouble, in River City or anywhere else. Get rid of them as soon as you can.

one you're trying to pocket. The accidentally grazed ball may make the cue ball behave erratically, and the grazed ball may get into the path of your next shot and ruin your strategy.

Whatever part of the table you're working, clear off the balls that spell trouble. They're easy enough to identify. They may be clustered together near a rail, away from the rack at the foot of the table, or in some other location in such a way that you know you've got problems. Even if it means changing your game plan, get rid of those balls, or they'll give you trouble later in the game when you might be getting set to go off on a run. You don't want to have to break open anything then, so get rid of those trouble balls now.

Here's a tip about one kind of trouble ball: if the object ball is frozen to a cushion, hit the cue ball so that it hits the cushion and the object ball simultaneously.

By the way, as nice as it is to have long runs (I've gone as high as 321 in an exhibition), sometimes, for defensive reasons, you're better off giving up the chance at a big run. A consistent 50 or 60 is much better than an occasional 100.

When you miss a shot, your inning ends. There's no penalty if the cue ball fails to hit the designated object ball, provided the cue ball hits at least one other ball and drives it into a cushion or a pocket, or the cue ball itself hits a cushion after contacting an object ball.

You realize, of course, that when your cue ball goes into a pocket it's a *scratch,* and you lose a point.

What some new players don't realize is that it's also a scratch if the cue ball goes off the table, or fails to hit another ball, or if both cue ball and object ball fail to hit a rail unless a ball is pocketed.

There are ways to avoid scratching: Sometimes, to prevent your cue ball from following the object ball into the pocket, you can hit the cue ball below center to draw it back. Do this even on an easy, straight-in shot. You can hit the cue ball dead center without its going into the pocket, just so long as you don't hit it very hard and you make it glance off the object ball at a slight angle. If the cue ball is lined up straight with the pocket, hit the object ball a little to one side. If the object ball is at an angle, hit the cue ball off to the side of the object ball that's away from the pocket. How hard you should hit it depends on how far you are from the object ball and whether or not you're playing for position.

There will be times when you'll want to scratch deliberately. Each time you do it will cost you a point, but it may be worth it when you're faced with a particularly difficult situation and you'd rather have your opponent break open a cluster of balls. If you scratch three times in a row, you lose an extra 15 points! Incredible as it may seem, there are times when *you'd be better off to take three scratches in a row* at the outset of a game and start with a minus-18 score than to open with a break that scatters the balls all over and gives your opponent wide-open shots.

Without meaning to scratch, you frequently will want to play a safety—a shot you take deliberately to leave the balls safe or tough for an opponent, without trying to make a point. You sacrifice your turn in order to leave your opponent with a next-to-impossible shot. You should do this when you either don't have a shot you can make or don't have the confidence you can make a shot open to you. If you do decide to play a safety, there are certain things to remember.

If you don't pocket the object ball, you either have to make the cue ball contact a cushion after it strikes the object ball or have to drive the object ball to another cushion. Otherwise you'll scratch and lose a point (or more, if it's your third in a row).

Irving Crane, a super defensive player who could and would beat you with his brain, was probably the best safety player there ever was.

We were playing in Illinois in a match in which I thought I had him beaten. He had the balls racked up and was frozen on the upper rail. He wanted to have the cue ball glance off the balls and come back up the table. He tried a two-cushion safety and missed. Deliberately, I just tapped the cue ball and left him safe on the bottom rail. Crane tried his safety shot again, and again he missed. Once more I tapped the cue ball and left him safe on the bottom rail.

I never dreamed he'd try that safety shot a third time in a

This is a *safe,* in which the cue ball is frozen into the stack and you don't have a clear shot. What should you do? Play another safe.

row. After all, he already had two consecutive scratches, costing him two points. If he scratched a third time, he'd lose 16 more points (1 for the scratch and 15 for the penalty for making three scratches in a row). But he did try the shot, and it was probably the most spectacular safety shot he ever made on me. Crane hit it perfectly and left me absolutely nothing.

It shook me up so much that I missed the next shot. Crane then coolly ran about 45 or 50 and put himself in a position to win the game. He beat me with his brain.

After he made the brilliant shot I said to him, "That was a heck of a safety with two scratches on you."

"I try, son," Crane said. "I try."

As much as I've been emphasizing playing safe, I must remind you that pocket billiards is a game you may never get a chance to shoot. Your opponent may keep scoring until he wins, without your having even one inning.

## Key Ball/Break Ball

The reason the game is called 14:1 Continuous is that after 14 of the object balls have been pocketed the 15th ball stays on the table as the *break ball*. The 14 pocketed balls are then racked up, and the game continues.

You can't have a high run, and you stand very little chance of winning games against good competition, if you can't make a break shot.

The *key ball* is the next-to-last ball left on the table before the balls are reracked.

When several balls are left, decide which is going to be the break shot and which is going to be the key shot. Pick as your break ball the one that is relatively close to where the triangle of balls will be set. Remember, the farther the cue ball has to travel, the more difficult the shot will be.

Assuming you've sunk the key ball, you would then go after the break ball. Ideally, you would make the break ball in a designated pocket and have the cue ball carom from the break

In this typical break shot in 14:1 you have run off 14 balls and left one on the table. The remaining balls have been reracked.

ball into the triangle of racked balls. Or you might have the cue ball carom from the break ball into one or more cushions and then into the rack.

After the key ball has been pocketed you are not obligated to shoot at the break ball. You might want to play safe by shooting into the rack instead. But remember that you've got to pocket a ball, drive an object ball to a cushion, or make the cue ball hit a cushion after contacting an object ball.

A good gauge of your progress is whether or not, after several months of play, you can run 15 or more balls in a row. If so, it means you made 14 and then, when the balls were reracked, you got into position to make the break shot.

## ONE-POCKET

In One-Pocket you and your opponent each select a pocket to be your own before the game begins. You should probably select one of the pockets at the foot of the table, since that's where the balls are likely to go on the break.

The object of the game is to sink eight balls into your pocket before your opponent sinks eight into his or hers.

Balls are racked in the triangle at random. They don't have to be played in any particular order, and you don't have to call those you're trying to sink.

### Tips

This is a game in which defensive play is crucial. Like a good chess player, you have to think four or five turns ahead. Even as you're taking the offensive, think and play defensively to leave your opponent the hardest bank shots imaginable. Don't take gambles because you'll probably lose.

It's unlikely that you will be able to make a ball in your pocket on the break. So, if you have to break, hit a safe break, a shot that will get as many balls near your pocket as possible without leaving your opponent a clear shot on his. You can do this by splitting the first two balls at the top of the triangle and trying to keep the ball over at your side.

Good strategy in this situation in One-Pocket is for you to bank the object ball (the 12-ball shown near the corner pocket at the top of the photo) over to your pocket (the corner pocket at the bottom of the photo).

If you're successful, it will put your opponent on the defensive. He or she will have to get balls away from your pocket or run the risk that you'll sink them. Your opponent will have to protect herself or himself at all times.

Obviously, though, two can play at the same game. If your opponent is skillful, you're not going to be left with any straight-in shots. So carom and bank shots are an important part of this game. But they take a lot of skill, and I don't recommend them until your game is well developed.

The 12-ball will start to come back toward your pocket. The cue ball will hit the side cushion (at the top of the above photo), come back, and be snookered between the 8-ball and the other object ball toward the top of the photo below.

## NINE-BALL

Of all the games played on a pool table, Nine-Ball is the number-one money game. It's fast and furious—money exchanges hands very quickly—so it's the game that all the pool hustlers prefer.

But you don't have to be a hustler, or even a particularly good player, to bet on Nine-Ball and enjoy it. I've seen everything from 25¢ to $1,000 wagered on a single Nine-Ball game.

A friend of mine and I once played Nine-Ball in Pittsburgh. We each put up $2,500, with the winner to take all—$5,000 takedown.

For the game of Nine-Ball, balls 1–9 are racked up in diamond formation, with the 9-ball in the middle and the 1-ball at the apex of the diamond.

We made the competition Five-Ahead, which means that the first one of us to get five games ahead of the other would win the money. Three times I got four games ahead, but I couldn't manage to pull off the victory. Then I got tired and weak, and he came back to beat me. It took six hours of playing before we reached the decision.

The rules of Nine-Ball are simple. As you can tell from the name, the object is to sink the 9-ball; whoever manages it first according to the rules wins the game.

A new rule has been introduced for Nine-Ball tournaments (as well as Eight-Ball and Seven-Ball) that makes the game very nerve-wracking and more interesting. It stipulates that anytime after the break, if you scratch in the pocket, or you don't hit the ball you're aiming at, your opponent gets the cue ball in hand *anywhere on the table.* He used to get the cue ball in hand behind the head string, but now it's anywhere on the table—obviously a big advantage. (On the break, it's still cue ball in hand but behind the head string.)

The rule was designed to accommodate TV viewers, to speed up the game, and to make it more interesting. With all the safeties that players are likely to use, the game could drag on a long time. The new rule accelerates play and somehow makes it more understandable.

## The Setup

To start the contest, balls 1 through 9 are placed in a diamond shape at the foot of the table, with the 1-ball at the head of the diamond facing the shooter and the 9-ball in the middle. The other seven balls are placed at random within the diamond shape.

The player who leads off tries to break the balls wide open and sink a ball. Then, starting with the 1-ball, he tries to pocket the balls in numerical order until he misses, or sinks the 9-ball, in which case he wins. Shots don't have to be called.

A player can sink the 9-ball on a combination and win, provided he also hits the balls he's aiming at (the one that's next in numerical rotation). For example, let's say the 1-ball has already been pocketed, which means the 2-ball is the one you have to try to sink next. Should you hit the 2-ball (with the cue ball) and knock the 2-ball into the 9-ball, pocketing the 9-ball, you'd win.

## Tips

Nine-Ball is one game where the break is all-important. If you make a ball on the break, you might win the game before your opponent even gets a chance to shoot. It's even possible that on the break you'll sink that 9-ball, which is buried in the middle of the diamond as play begins.

I once played a series of four-handed games of Nine-Ball, in which the players picked numbered pills to determine the order in which they'd shoot, and I didn't get a chance to shoot for 12 games! Then, when I finally did get a chance to shoot, I didn't get a good shot, and I went another 12 games without a chance. Believe me, that's mighty frustrating.

No matter how many players are involved, if you're lucky enough to be the player who's going to break, you should place the white cue ball just a few inches to the right side of the head spot. Hit the cue ball with a good solid shot, with the cue stick making contact about a cue tip's distance above the center, and aim the cue ball smack at the center of the front ball in the rack. Then hope. Hope you wallop the balls in the diamond so that you pocket one or more of them—maybe, if your rabbit's foot is working, the 9-ball itself. I want to emphasize that making the 9-ball on the break is sheer luck.

On the break in Nine-Ball, it's important that the cue ball doesn't run wild all over the table because, if you scratch (pocketing the cue ball), your opponent takes over, and there's a good chance he'll go all the way for a win. This chance is especially good if you're playing with the rule that he or she gets the cue ball in hand anywhere on the table.

I watched two players compete in Virginia for $2,000 in a

session of Nine-Ball. (A session is a set of 21 games, with the first player to win 11 games the victor.) One of those players won the break and scratched five times in a row! It goes without saying that that rash of scratches was very costly, and it must have left him itching.

Seriously, it's important to avoid scratching. The best way to avoid it is to try to control the cue ball so that it comes back to the center of the table after contact with the balls in the diamond. That's why I suggested you hit the cue ball about a tip's distance above the center.

There are two basically different ways of playing Nine-Ball: Hit-the-Ball and One-Shot Shoot-Out. You and your opponent decide before you start playing which one you'll use. Here are the ways the differences show up.

Suppose you're snookered (there's a ball in the way of the one you want to hit). In Hit-the-Ball you've got to take an honest try at the ball. In One-Shot Shoot-Out you're allowed to stroke the cue ball so that it doesn't hit anything, without being penalized.

In this case, you're trying to hit the cue ball to a part of the table where, even if the object ball could be "seen" (that is, where the path from the cue ball to object ball is clear), you'd still leave your opponent with only a very difficult shot.

If you do that, your opponent has the option of trying to make that tough shot or declaring that he wants *you* to try it. If he lets you take it, and you miss hitting a ball—that would be the second time in a row you've missed—your opponent gets the cue ball in hand anywhere he wants. This is a very bad thing to let happen because it gives him an excellent chance of winning the game on this turn.

On the other hand, if your opponent had decided to risk that tough shot you left him, and he missed the designated ball, *you* would get the cue ball in hand.

There is no limit on how many times a player can hit the cue ball to make a hard shot for his opponent without hitting an object ball, just as long as he doesn't do it on two shots in a row.

Big bettors tend to prefer One-Shot Shoot-Out, which provides more protection and greater defense. Smaller bettors, those who play for $5 or $10, generally like Hit the Ball, which is more exciting because you never know where the balls will wind up.

Nine-Ball can be played with two, three, four, or five players. Sometimes the game played with four or five is called Ring Nine-Ball. When you're competing against a lot of players you've got to be lucky in drawing the number that determines where in the order you'll play. If you're not lucky, you might be up against what I mentioned earlier, not getting a shot for a dozen games.

All games played on a pool table are tough. A game like Nine-Ball, in which object balls have to be pocketed in a designated order, is a little tougher.

One reason Nine-Ball is a favorite of hustlers is that they can easily disguise themselves to look a little bit like bad players, until they get the bet up to a substantial sum. In Nine-Ball every single brief game is a different one, so the hustler can lose a few quickly, as opposed to Straight Pool, where it's continuous, thus making it harder for the hustler to catch up.

A hustler will get into a four-hand game of Nine-Ball and deliberately play like a bum for a while. Thinking he's a real sucker, his opponents will want to bet more money. Then, when the ante gets good and high, the hustler proceeds to wipe them out.

As a spectator, if you have some inside information or inkling that one of the players is a hustler, he's the one you should bet on. If you're really sly, you'll hold off your wager until the time seems ripe for the hustler to make his move.

If you don't suspect any player of being a hustler, bet on the one who seems to have the edge in skill or confidence. Otherwise, just take your chances, as you would in any form of gambling.

But better yet, get into the game yourself. Nine-Ball is exciting—and potentially profitable—for any pool player, regardless of his or her level of play.

A strategic move in playing Nine-Ball is to drive the object ball off the rail and up the table and leave your opponent snookered behind an object ball (the 8-ball in this case). The 5-ball you had a shot at would have been a tough shot. So you make it wind up beyond the 9-ball past the side pocket. Your opponent is snookered behind the 8-ball. He has to kick off the side rail and hope he hits his ball. If he doesn't, you get the cue ball in hand, and you're a big favorite to win. In Nine-Ball, try to keep snookering your opponent until you get an easy shot.

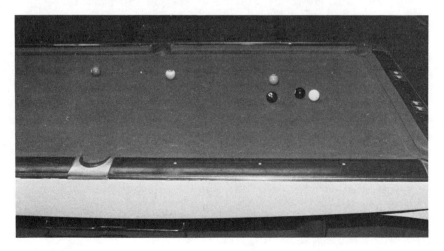

## EIGHT-BALL

So many things can go wrong in this game that you'll find yourself trying as hard not to do something that will make you lose the game as to do things to win it.

The object is to pocket a specific seven of the 15 object balls and then the 8-ball before your opponent does his or hers. The 8-ball must be saved for last.

One player has to pocket balls 1 through 7 before sinking the 8-ball; the other, 9 through 15.

The 15 object balls are racked up in the triangle with the 8-ball in the center.

On the break, drive the cue ball as hard as you can to sink whatever balls you can. If you pocket one or more balls on the break, you choose balls numbered either 1–7 or 9–15, and your opponent is assigned the category you don't select. If you don't pocket any, your opponent gets the choice.

If your opponent breaks and doesn't sink any balls, see which category has the most balls within easy-shot range of a pocket and choose that category as yours.

You don't have to call any shots, except the one involving the 8-ball. You get credit for all balls you pocket legally. If you should accidentally sink a competitor's ball, he or she gets credit for it. You lose your turn and he or she gets up to shoot. If you sink your ball as well as your opponent's, you continue shooting but your opponent still gets credit for his or her ball.

You *win* the game if you pocket the 8-ball on the opening break.

But you *lose* the game if
- you pocket the 8-ball before you've pocketed all seven of your numbered balls;
- you're trying to make the 8-ball and it goes into a different pocket from the one you designated;
- you're shooting for the 8-ball but on that shot the cue ball hits another ball before the 8-ball is pocketed;
- you're shooting to make the 8-ball, and the cue ball scratches in a pocket.

You can see how easy it is to end up "behind the 8-ball."

Sorry to report, you're behind the 8-ball. In the game of Eight-Ball, when you've got just one of your balls left on the table, there's a good chance you're going to be behind the 8-ball. Here, the 8-ball blocks your cue from your object ball.

### Tip

Try to make your set of balls without breaking up clusters or any type of trouble balls that could cause problems for your opponent.

## SEVEN-BALL

The up-and-coming pool sensation, in my opinion, is Seven-Ball, a game that can be enjoyed by novice and pro alike. It has some similarity to Nine-Ball, but has a character all its own.

The object is to make the 7-ball in a pocket on your side of the table (after balls 1–6 have been pocketed).

After the break the player who does not break decides which side will be his or hers and which will be the opponent's.

Only balls 1–7 are used. For the break, you rack balls 1–6 in a

For the game of Seven-Ball, balls 1–6 are racked in a circle, with the 1-ball at the apex and the 7-ball in the middle of the circle. All balls touch one another.

circle, with the 7-ball in the middle. The 1-, 2-, and 3-balls are on one side of the circle; the 4-, 5-, and 6-balls are on the other. If your opponent breaks, fails to pocket a ball, and leaves the 7-ball near the right side of the table, of course, you'll choose the pockets on that side as your own. Even if your opponent makes a ball on the break, you get to pick the side you want. (There are variations on the game, such as having only one pocket on a side or on the whole table designated for the 7-ball.)

The game is so new that pros are undecided about whether or not it's an advantage to break.

The only scratch in the game occurs when the cue ball goes into the pocket.

The key to the game is maneuvering the 7-ball. If you can position it so that it's in the jaw of one of your pockets, your opponent just isn't going to be able to win. If he or she hits that ball into your pocket, you win. Thus, much of the strategy necessarily revolves around getting the 7-ball to your side of the table.

You can win the game by pocketing the 7-ball before the others have been made, as long as you make a correct hit on the right ball first. Suppose the 1- and 2-balls have been pocketed, and you're aiming to hit the 3-ball. If the cue ball hits the 3-ball, and the 3-ball drives the 7-ball into your pocket, you win.

# 7
# Trick Shots

Now for the really fun part of pocket billiards—trick shots.

The best trick shot artist in the world was probably Charley Peterson. He knew more than 200 trick shots and could put on an exhibition for more than two hours without ever showing you the same trick twice.

From Peterson on down to the rawest novice, trick shots require the same elements. They come with practice and depend mainly on the setup.

Sometimes even professionals, myself included, don't set the balls up properly for a trick shot. So you reset them and try again.

Do your best to set the balls up properly for your trick shots, but don't get discouraged if you don't make them the first, second, or even third time, especially if you're a novice. I've been shooting pool for 30 years, and I can't make every one on the first or second attempt. It's really a matter of trial and error, so keep trying.

In the pages that follow I've included more than two dozen trick shots, ranging from very easy to very tough. Some of the

Here I give a twisted, reassuring smile as I prepare to dazzle nonbelievers with some trick shots.

shots—mainly the ones in which all you have to do is hit the cue ball straight, without English or anything fancy—can be made by anybody. Other shots—say, where the cue ball has to make a complete circle or arc on the table—can be made only by a player with relatively good skills. Both types demand proper setup.

I've labeled the tricks *easy, tricky,* or *very tricky* (depending on how hard they are to set up) and *tough* or *very tough* (depending on how hard the shot is to make). Some of the trick shots appear easy but are difficult, and vice versa. With experience, you'll be able to make almost all of them look easy. For the time being, though, you'll be able to do only some. So don't get discouraged. Just be careful to set them up right, stroke as ordered—and have a ball.

Let's start with some easy tricks.

## THROUGH THE BAG

### The Setup

Place a small paper bag, preferably a new one, on the table, lined up with the right corner pocket at the foot of the table. It

## Through the Bag

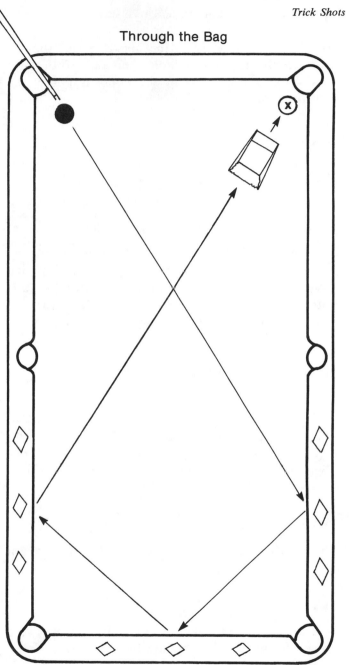

should be about 18 inches from the pocket. Open the bag at the top, which faces away from the hole. Spread it so that a ball can get into it. Place the cue ball at the opposite corner pocket at the foot of the table.

### The Stroke

Aiming toward the head of the table, hit the cue ball with a medium stroke with high right-hand English.

### The Result

The cue ball should hit the second diamond on the right side from the head of the table, carom to the middle diamond at the head cushion and the third diamond on the left-hand rail, before going into the bag. The momentum will turn the bag over, the pocket. (Remember, angles may vary with the table and amount of English.)

## FIVE IN ONE (OR FOUR AND ONE)

### The Setup

Line up four object balls at a right angle to one side pocket. They should be *frozen* (touching each other). Then place a fifth object ball at the opposite side pocket. Place the point of the triangle against object ball A.

### The Stroke

Hit the middle of the cue ball with a medium stroke into the middle of the back of the rack.

### The Result

You will pocket all four balls in one side pocket. The cue ball will bounce off the rack and make object ball B in the opposite side pocket.

## Five in One

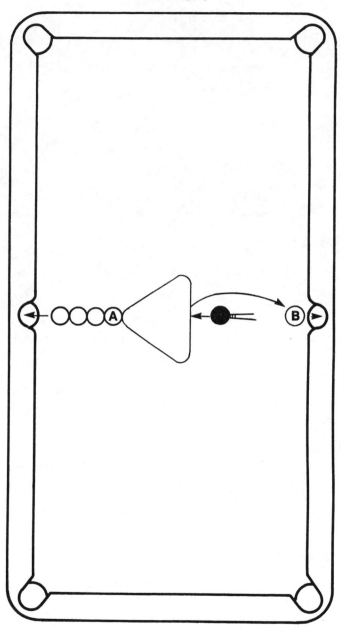

For the Lazy Man Rack trick, I put 14 object balls in a triangle and have the cue ball lift the triangle up at the point. I drive the remaining object ball off three cushions, and—voila!—the object ball knocks the cue ball away and moves neatly into place in the rack as the triangle comes down.

## THE LAZY MAN RACK

### The Setup

Place 14 object balls into the triangle as shown and place the cue ball underneath the triangle to raise it.

### The Stroke

Stroke object ball X (which is outside the triangle) into the second diamond at the opposite side of the table toward the foot. Use high right-hand English with a medium stroke.

## Lazy Man Rack

### The Result

The object ball will hit three cushions and knock the cue ball away. The triangle will fall into place with the object ball at the apex in perfect formation.

## BROKEN PYRAMID

### The Setup

Have the cue ball at the head spot. Place the pyramid of balls at the foot spot in the usual formation, except that ball X is removed from the point and placed behind and between the third and fourth ball in the rear row.

### The Stroke

Hit the cue ball with a medium stroke, giving it high right-hand English. Aim for the second diamond toward the foot of the table where balls 1 and 2 are located.

### The Result

The cue ball will carom off that cushion, hit the foot cushion, and then hit the side of object ball X, which is frozen against balls 3 and 4. Object ball X should then make it to the far right pocket.

## ON THE ENDS

Sometimes a good pool trick shooter has to be a little pushy, as in the following.

### The Setup

Freeze the cue ball and three object balls on the head rail, with the cue ball at the first diamond from the left corner pocket.

## Broken Pyramid

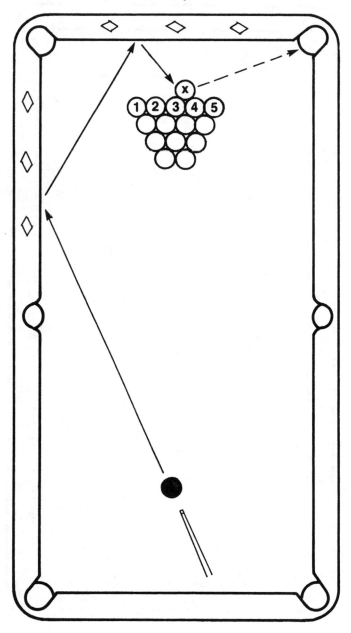

## On the Ends

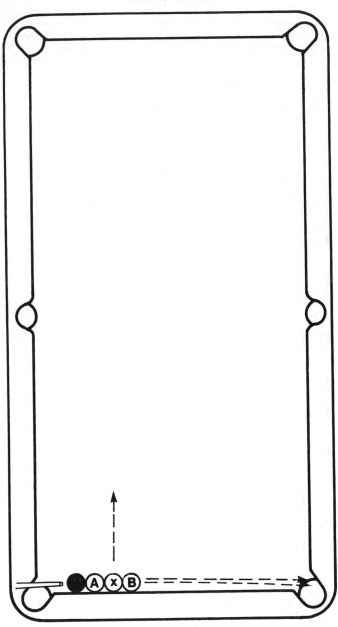

## The Stroke

Put the tip of the cue on the cue ball with high left-hand English and, rather than shoot, *push* the cue.

## The Result

Balls A and B will go into the right corner pocket, while ball X moves out.

## THE ONE IN THE MIDDLE

How do you get one ball to come out of the middle of a cluster and go into a pocket while those around it stay put? Easy, if you know how.

## The Setup

Line up object balls A, B, and C frozen to each other and to the head rail, beginning about a foot in from the left corner pocket. Have the cue ball frozen to ball A at about the 10 o'clock position.

## The Stroke

Place the cue tip against the cue ball and, instead of shooting, *push* with high right-hand English, making the cue tip go toward the cushion.

## The Result

Balls A and C go up while B goes straight through to right corner pocket.

Text continues on page 106.

## One in the Middle

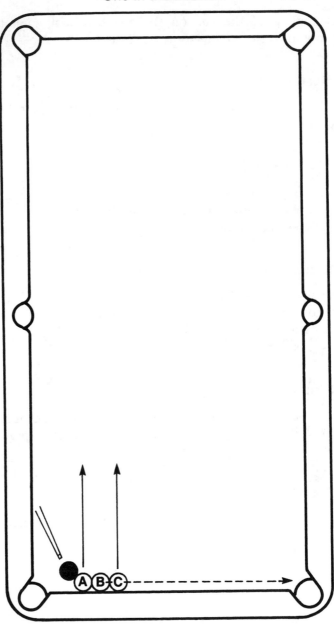

## Out of the Rack

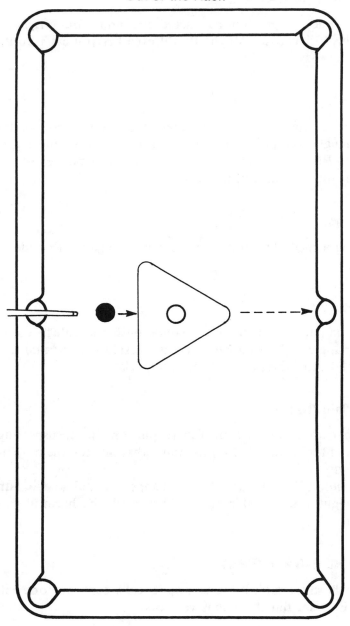

## OUT OF THE RACK

This one shapes up as incredible, and your friends will probably tell you so. Maybe they'll even bet you can't do it. But it's really easy.

### The Setup

Place an object ball in the center of the table, in the middle of the triangle, the point of which is aiming toward the right side pocket. Place the cue ball near the left side pocket so that it aims at the midpoint of the rack.

### The Shot

Using a medium stroke, hit the cue ball against the side of the triangle.

### The Result

The impact will make the triangle push the ball to the front. The triangle will be pushed toward the side pocket, and the ball will fall out of the rack and into the pocket.

### Just Plain Rotten

Two trick shots that are fun to pull on the unsuspecting are downright rotten. That's probably what makes them so much fun to do.

*Warning:* If your friends are temperamental and/or strong, you might want to skip these. They could be harmful to your health.

## HIT THE 8-BALL FIRST

They'll say it can't be done, and it really can't be done without body English. But this one is very easy.

# Hit the 8-Ball First

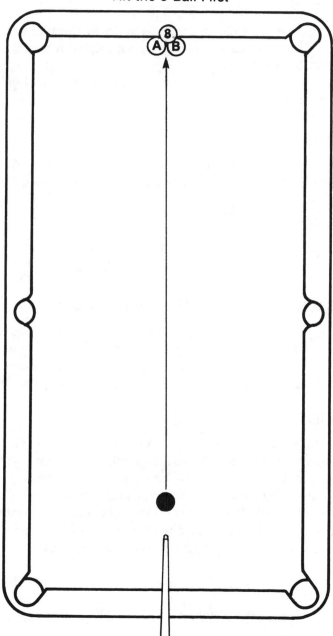

### The Setup

Place two object balls, A and B, frozen to the foot rail at the middle diamond. Place the 8-ball on top of the foot rail so that it leans on balls A and B.

Then claim that you will make the cue ball hit the 8-ball first. They'll never believe you.

### The Stroke

Just shoot the cue ball right in between object balls A and B, at the same time discreetly bumping the table with your body.

### The Result

The object balls A and B will move out of the way, and the 8-ball will fall to the table, where it will be hit by the cue ball.

## CUE BALL IN THE LEFT-HAND SIDE POCKET

Before you try this, I'd suggest you make sure you have your life insurance paid up. It's just that sneaky. But it's possible to do what you claim: put the cue ball into the left side pocket, after making balls A and B in their respective corner pockets.

### The Setup

Place object ball A and object ball B at opposite ends of the head rail in the jaws of the corner pockets and lay a cue stick across so that it touches both balls, as shown. Place your cue ball about a foot from the left rail and about 8 to 10 inches from the cue stick lying on the table. To make the shot seem even more impossible, place object balls C and D so that they seem to be guarding all but a narrow opening at the left side pocket.

### The Stroke

Hit the center of the cue ball with a hard stroke, driving it to the foot rail.

## Cue Ball in the Left-Hand Side Pocket

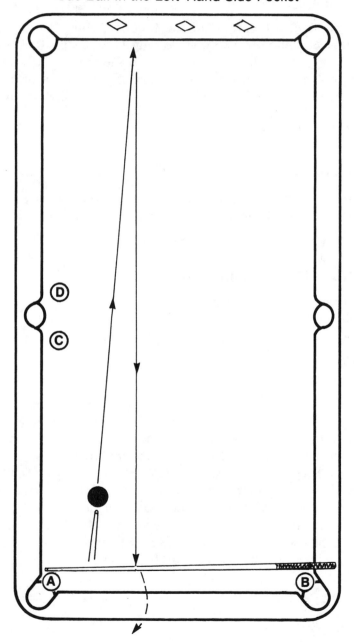

### The Result

The cue ball will carom off the foot rail, come back, and hit the cue stick lying on the table, forcing balls A and B into their pockets. The cue ball will then vault off the table. Catch the cue ball and place it in the left-hand pocket of your jacket or pants.

(Another result is that the people you're showing off to may pick up the cue stick and drive *you* into a side pocket.)

Balls C and D were just decoys!

### Three Not-So-Easy Pieces

Here are three trick shots that will have your friends muttering in their beer. They look so very easy, but they aren't—unless you know the gimmick.

## MY KID SISTER COULD MAKE THAT

No offense to young women is intended by this name; the shot is called that because that's the normal reaction most fellows have when they're challenged to try the trick.

### The Setup

Place ball A about 10 inches from the right side pocket and freeze balls B and C to A, as shown. Then tell your (former) friend to put the cue ball wherever he wants and pocket ball A. Odds are he'll leave the cue ball in the middle because the shot looks so easy from that setup. But not so fast, my friend. It's almost impossible that way. Let your friend try several times. Then when he gives up, you demonstrate how easy it is.

Place the cue ball, as shown, near the left-hand rail at the head of the table. Line it up so that an imaginary line from the left corner pocket through the cue ball would hit the left side of ball C.

## My Kid Sister Could Make That

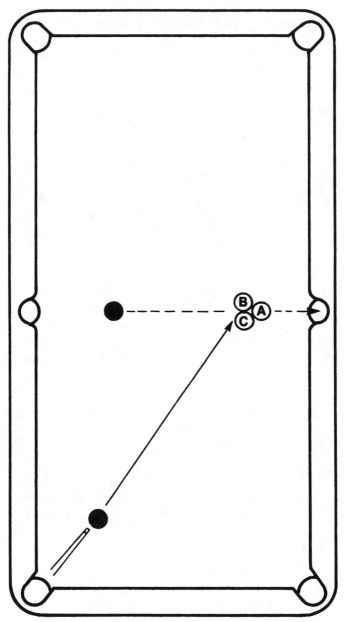

### The Stroke

Hit the cue ball with top left-hand English, aiming at the left side of ball C.

### The Result

The cue ball will just kiss ball C and glance into ball B, which will bang ball A into the pocket.

Knowing how it works, your friend's kid sister—or even your friend—can do it.

## KNOCK DOWN THE MATCH

If you don't want to set the world on fire but just want to set a flame (of envy) in the heart of your friend, challenge him or her to knock down the match. This is a very tough shot.

### The Setup

Split the bottom of a paper match to give it a flat surface to stand on. Then wet the head spot and stand the match on it. Form a triangle of three balls—A, B, and C—around the match, making sure they're kissing. Put the cue ball into the center of the table and invite your friend to try to knock the match down. What will probably happen is that he or she will hit the cue ball as hard as possible. Even with a direct hit, the match will just stand there, unimpressed. You're perfectly within your rights to wisecrack a little about your big, strong friend's inability to knock down a tiny match.

### The Stroke

When you shoot, put as much follow on the cue ball as you can, so that the cue ball will continue to spin forward.

### The Result

The match should go down. To get the message across that brain has triumphed over brawn, just silently tap your temple with your index finger.

## Knock Down the Match

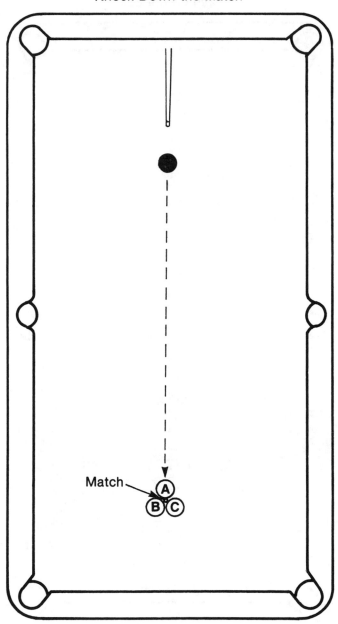

## Coin on the Ball

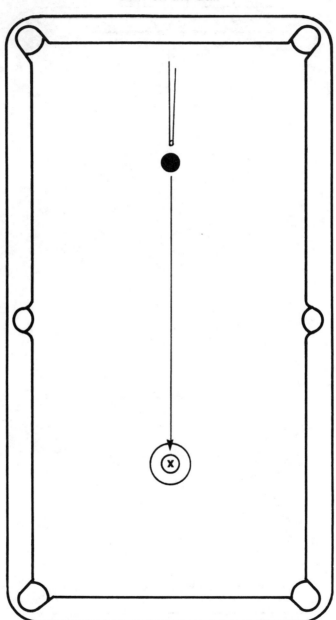

## THE COIN ON THE BALL

You can invest two bits or a half-dollar in this trick and win a small bundle.

### The Setup

Put an object ball on the head spot and then take chalk and make a circle around the ball about eight inches in diameter. Then put one of your hard-earned quarters or half-dollars on top of the ball. Place the cue ball behind the foot string and challenge your friend to try to knock the coin out of the circle. The natural inclination will be to hit the cue ball as hard as possible. The only trouble is that that way the coin won't leave the circle.

### The Stroke

After your frustrated friend gives up and it's your turn, either hit the cue ball extremely slowly or hit it head-on with follow.

### The Result

When you hit the cue ball very slowly, the coin rolls off the object ball. When you hit it head-on, the cue ball knocks the coin out of the circle.

Not that I'd ever do something that devious, but some players have been known to hustle their opponents with this shot.

Now, here are some tricky tricks.

## BE CAREFUL

This trick requires something of a *wet*-and-see attitude.

### The Setup

Freeze object balls B and C to each other and to the right-

## Be Careful

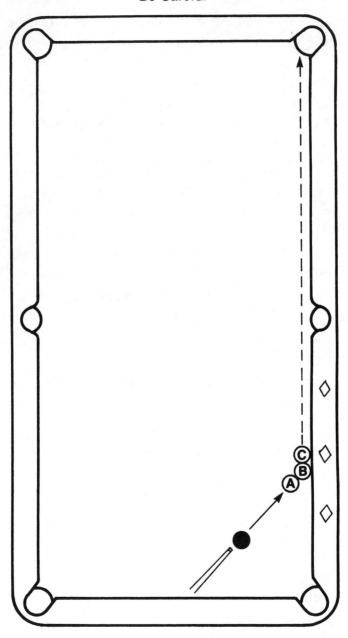

hand rail near the second diamond. Freeze ball A to ball B at about the 7 o'clock position.

More important than the stroke is preparing the contact point between balls B and C by wetting it. Performing this trick shot is more a matter of knowing a basic fact of physics than anything else. Unless you wet the contact point, the balls will be affected by the English you apply to the cue ball, forcing ball C into the rail. If you do wet it, the effect of the English will be negated.

## The Stroke

Hit the center of the cue ball with a moderate stroke, driving it into ball A.

## The Result

The impact will drive ball C to the desired corner pocket.

## ALL AROUND THE TABLE

Only a bad shot can keep the cue ball from making its appointed rounds in this trick. If it does the job, three balls will find pockets to land in.

## The Setup

Freeze object balls A and B to each other, at a right angle to the right-hand rail and frozen to that rail. They should be near the right side pocket but not quite in line with it. Place object ball C near the left corner pocket at the head of the table. Place the cue ball opposite the third diamond on the right rail at the head of the table, about six inches in from the rail.

## The Stroke

Use high right-hand English and a medium stroke to make the cue ball strike one-quarter of ball A.

## All Around the Table

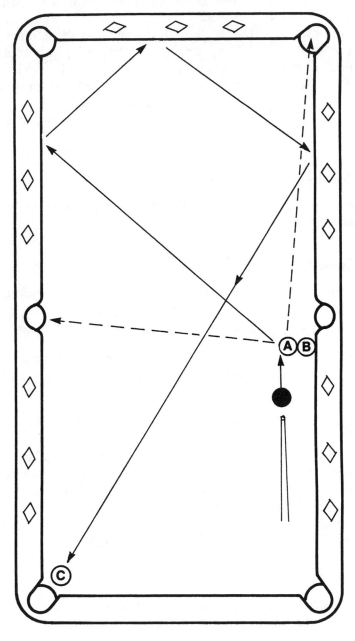

## The Result

Ball A will go into the right corner pocket at the foot of the table while ball B banks across the table to the left side pocket. The cue ball will hit three cushions and knock ball C into the left corner pocket at the head of the table.

## WHICH ONE GOES?

Ask the skeptics to guess which one of these many object balls goes into the pocket. (The answer, just for your benefit, is ball D.) This trick sets things in motion in an incredible way.

## The Setup

At about where the first diamond is located, set up a wall of five balls, frozen to one another. Ball A is at the right and ball C at the left. Leave a couple of inches of space and then place balls B and D behind A and C, respectively. Have balls B and D frozen to a row of three frozen balls. Place the cue ball between the first diamond to the right of the head rail and the center diamond.

## The Stroke

Use a hard stroke on the center of the cue ball, toward ball A.

## The Result

Ball C will go to the rail, ball A will hit ball B, and the momentum will travel all the way to ball D, which will be driven to the corner pocket. (Ball D should be aimed on the dotted line.)

Text continues on page 122.

## Which One Goes?

## Off the Point

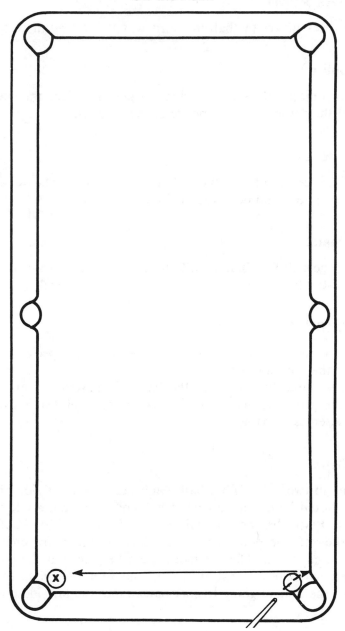

## OFF THE POINT

This trick makes the ball the hard way. It's a legitimate shot.

### The Setup

Place object ball X at a corner pocket and place the cue ball behind the corner of the opposite corner pocket.

### The Stroke

Hit the center of the cue ball with an easy stroke so that it hits the opposite point of the pocket.

### The Result

The cue ball will bounce off the corner and travel across the head of the table to knock object ball X into the pocket.

## BLOCKBUSTER

Here's one guaranteed to impress everyone, especially members of the opposite sex.

Moses raised his staff and the Red Sea parted; if you stroke your cue properly, two rows of balls will miraculously part. This trick deserves its name.

### The Setup

Line up two rows of six balls each near the right side pocket. They should be frozen to each other and at a right angle to the pocket. Place the three remaining object balls—X, Y, and Z—near the left side pocket, in triangular formation, frozen to one another, as shown. The cue ball should be placed at the point of the left side pocket that is nearer the foot of the table. Announce that you're going to sink ball X into the far side pocket.

## Blockbuster

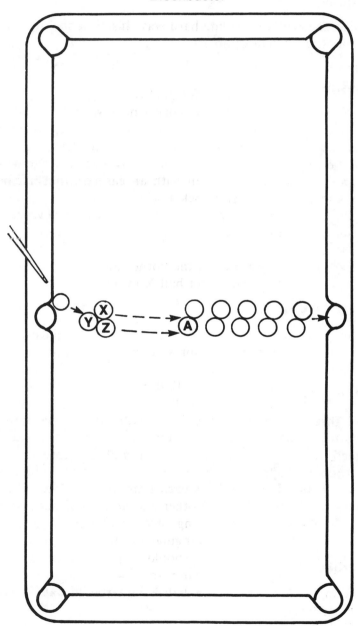

### The Stroke

Hit the cue ball very solidly, using high left-hand English, so that it hits the left half of object ball Y.

### The Result

Ball Y will be knocked out of the way toward the head rail. Ball Z will hit the right edge of ball A (the one nearest the center of the table in the row of balls closer to the head of the table). The impact will cause the rows of balls to separate with a clatter, and object ball X will roll down the path that has been cleared, straight into the right side pocket.

It helps to have a long arm. That way, you can give yourself a well deserved pat on the back.

Here are some very tricky tricks.

## UP AND DOWN

If you pull this one off, you'll amaze even the most cynical members of your audience.

### The Setup

Place three cue sticks so that their butts are jammed into the right corner pocket at the head of the table. Two of them should be aimed toward the left side pocket and be close together. Position object balls A and B at the side pocket and object ball C frozen to ball B at a right angle to the pocket. Place the cue ball near the left-hand rail about 10 inches to the head side of balls A, B, and C.

### The Stroke

Using high left-hand English, hit one-quarter of ball C with a medium stroke.

## Up and Down

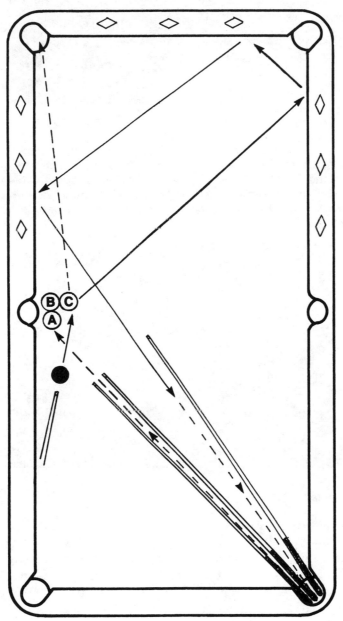

For the Up and Down trick, I lay three cue sticks on the table with their butts jammed into the right corner pocket at the head of the table. Two are together, separated from the third. With one shot I pocket two of the balls, cause the cue ball to travel three cushions and then go between the cue sticks toward the corner pocket, mount the rail around the corner pocket, come back along the crevice formed by the two cue sticks frozen together, and knock the remaining object ball into the left side pocket.

## The Result

The cue ball should carom off ball C, sending ball B into the side pocket and ball C into the left corner pocket at the foot of the table. The cue ball will carom from ball C to the right side rail just below the first diamond and go three cushions. It will then travel up between two of the cues, around the corner pocket, and back down through the middle and third cues to make object ball A in the side pocket.

## HANKY-PANKY

This trick is nothing to sneeze at, though it uses a handkerchief to disguise your object.

### The Setup

Place an object ball on the foot spot and cover it with a handkerchief. Place your cue ball a few inches from the left rail, about even with the second diamond.

### The Stroke

Aiming for the first diamond from the right at the foot rail, use a moderate stroke and hit the cue ball dead center.

### The Result

The hidden object ball should go into the right corner pocket at the foot of the table.

## FOUR IN ONE

Make sure you set up the balls absolutely frozen—and you'll make the shot cold.

### The Setup

Place object balls A and C, frozen to each other, right next to the right side pocket. Freeze ball D to ball A so that D faces the middle of the opposite corner pocket at the head of the table. Place ball B at the right corner pocket at the foot of the table.

### The Stroke

Using a medium draw stroke, hit the cue ball below center into the center of object ball A.

**Text continues on page 130.**

## Hanky Panky

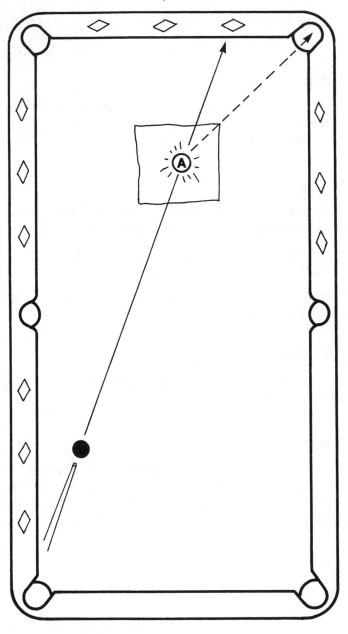

## Four in One

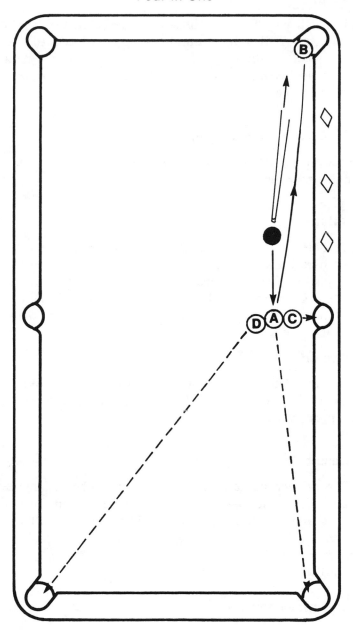

## The Result

Ball A will go into the right corner pocket at the head of the table, the cue ball will rebound and hit ball B into the right corner pocket at the foot of the table, while C goes into the right side pocket and D goes into the left corner pocket at the head of the table.

## THREE BALLS IN ROTATION

Here's another that doesn't look possible, but is—with a little luck and proper setup.

## The Setup

Place object ball A frozen to the cushion at the first diamond of the left rail near the head of the table. Freeze object ball B to ball A, just a trifle more toward the foot of the table, and freeze object ball C to object ball B. The cue ball should be about 16 inches from the left rail between the second and third diamonds.

## The Stroke

Using high left-hand English and a moderate stroke, hit the cue ball so that it contacts the left cushion and object ball A simultaneously.

## The Result

Ball A will be made in the left corner pocket at the head of the table. The cue ball caroms off the rail and into ball B, sending that into the same pocket and propelling ball C (which is automatically lined up properly) into the opposite corner pocket at the head of the table.

All three balls should go in.

Now for some tough ones.

# Three Balls in Rotation

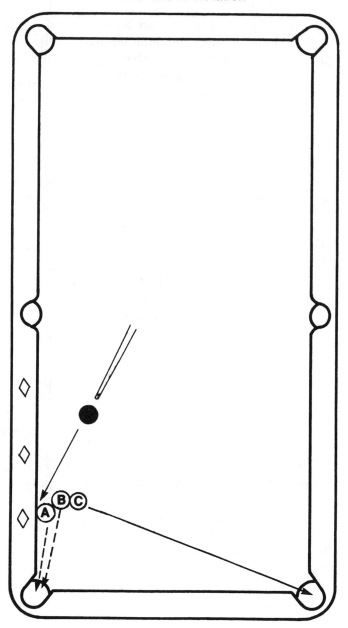

## Cheap Shot (50¢)

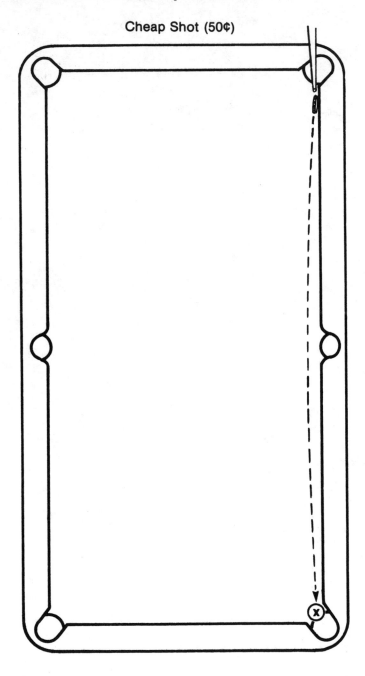

## CHEAP SHOT (50¢)

Remember that half-dollar you used for the coin-on-the-ball shot? Get it out of your pocket and put it to use one more time to impress your friends.

Boast that you're going to use the coin instead of the cue ball to sink an object ball. After the horselaughs die down, proceed as follows:

### The Setup

Put an object ball on the edge of the corner pocket. Then lean your half-dollar at the opposite end of the table against the side rail, on its edge.

### The Stroke

Strike the edge of the coin solidly with your cue stick.

### The Result

The coin will roll along the rail and knock the ball into the pocket.

It's really not that difficult. As your friends' mouths open, open yours to smirk. Then pocket (*your* pocket, that is) the half-dollar and any other currency that might have been put up to say, "You'll never do it."

## OVER THE CUE

This is a toughie with three possible variations. In each situation, stroke the same.

### Variation 1

### The Setup

Lay a cue stick diagonally from the third diamond on the left

## Over the Cue (Variation 1)

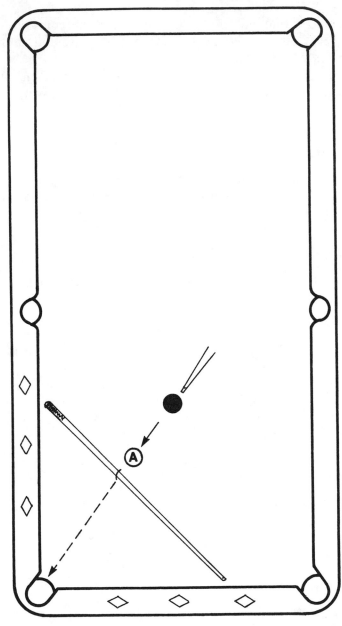

rail to the third diamond on the head rail. Place an object ball about six inches from the cue stick, lined up with the left corner pocket at the head of the table, but on the side of the stick away from the pocket. Place the cue ball about 12 inches behind the object ball, lined up with the object ball for the corner pocket.

## The Stroke

Elevate the butt of your cue, hit down on the cue ball with a medium stroke, and follow through.

## The Result

Object ball A will jump over the cue into the corner pocket.

## Variation 2

### The Setup

Place the object ball about six to eight inches from the cue stick but on the side of the stick *toward* the pocket. Place the cue ball about 12 inches from the cue stick on the side of the stick away from the pocket.

### The Stroke

Elevate the butt of your cue, hit down on the cue ball with a medium stroke, and follow through.

### The Result

The cue ball will jump over the cue, contact the object ball, and drive it into the corner pocket.

Text continues on page 138.

## Over the Cue (Variation 2)

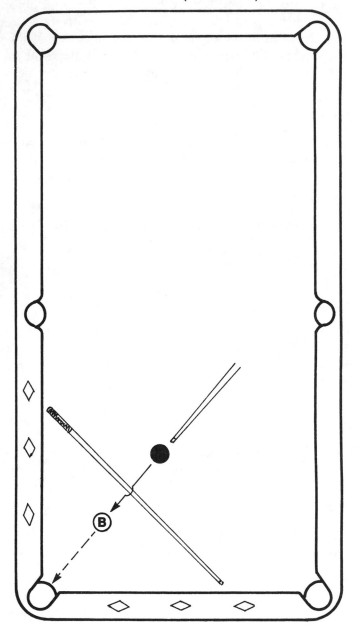

## Over the Cue (Variation 3)

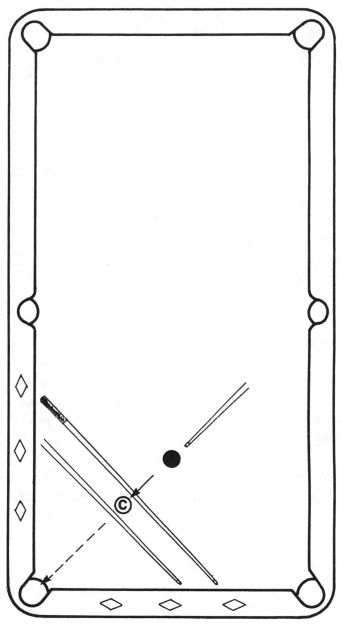

## Variation 3

### The Setup

Place a second cue stick parallel to the first, about 16 inches away. Place the object ball about halfway between the two sticks. Place the cue ball about 12 inches away from the stick that is farther from the hole.

### The Stroke

Elevate the butt of your cue, hit down on the cue ball with a medium stroke, and follow through.

### The Result

The cue ball will jump over the cue farther from the hole and strike the object ball, which will then jump over the stick closer to the pocket and continue into the pocket.

## ALONG THE RAIL

### The Setup

Place object ball A in the jaw of the right corner pocket at the foot of the table and object ball B in the opposite corner pocket at the foot of the table. Place the cue ball about halfway between the right corner pocket and the right side pocket, about six inches from the rail.

### The Stroke

Hold the cue level with the bed of the table. Hit the cue ball with high left-hand English, using a hard stroke, and follow through. Strike one-half of object ball A.

### The Result

The cue ball should then go across the table, hugging the foot rail, to put object ball B into the corner pocket.

## Along the Rail

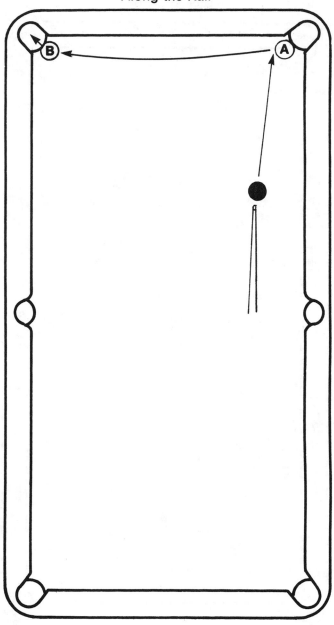

## Force Draw Shot

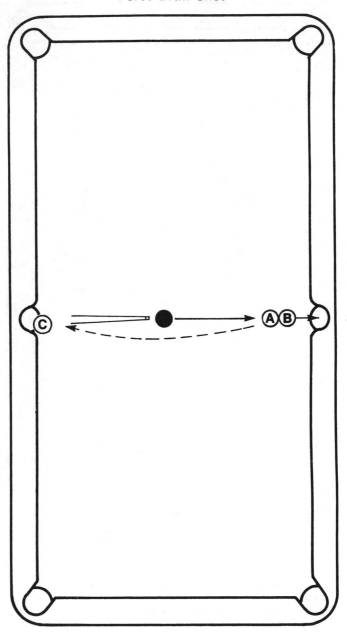

## FORCE DRAW SHOT

This one is a lot tougher than it looks, and it doesn't look that easy.

### The Setup

Place the cue ball in the center of the table. Have object balls A and B frozen to each other and lined up within the side pocket on the right rail. Place object ball C in the same line within the side pocket at the left rail.

### The Stroke

Aim the cue ball toward object ball A, using low center English to get a hard draw stroke.

### The Result

Ball A should follow ball B into one pocket. The cue ball will draw back across the table and hit ball C so that the object ball goes into that pocket.

## JUST SHOWIN' OFF—THE LITE BEER COMMERCIAL SHOT

When I really feel like showin' off, whether on a Lite commercial or in a heavy challenge at a billiard parlor, the biggie I shoot for is the one I call the Six in One. You, too, can dazzle your friends, stupefy your critics, and astound even yourself with this one, in which one shot sinks six balls.

### The Setup

Place the cue ball about 6 inches from the right side rail near the head of the table, opposite the middle diamond. Place ball F in the left corner near the head of the table, facing that left

## Just Showin' Off (Six in One)

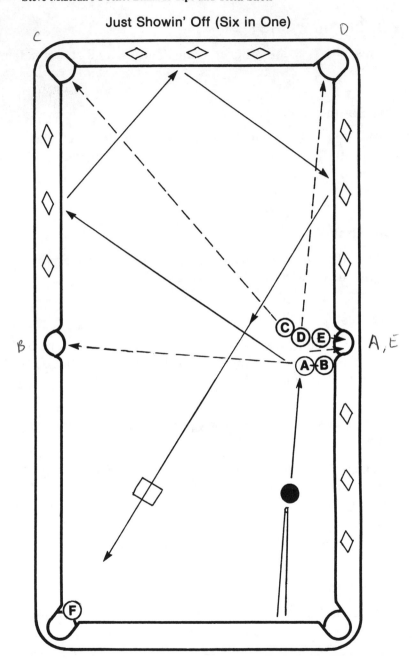

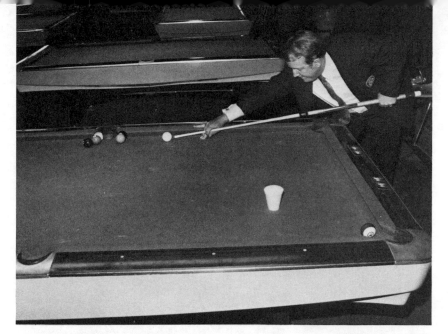

I'm preparing to shoot my famous "Just Showin' Off" trick shot. Five balls are located strategically near the right side pocket. A cup and a ball are placed near the left corner pocket at the head of the table. When I connect, the five object balls at the side will go into four different pockets. The cue ball will go off three cushions and then head for the left corner pocket.

corner pocket. Place balls A and B (frozen on the rail) about an inch down from the right side pocket, at a right angle to the pocket. These balls should not be opposite the pocket, but a shade toward the head rail. Place balls D and E at the middle of the right side pocket, frozen to each other, and set up ball C frozen to D and aiming at the upper point of the left corner pocket at the foot of the table.

Announce that you'll pocket all six object balls with one shot.

### The Stroke

Strike the cue ball solidly, using a lot of high right-hand English, into the left half of ball A.

### The Result

Ball A will go into the right side pocket. Its movement will cause ball B to travel across the table and into the left side

Just in time, I remove the cup from the path of the cue ball, which is heading to knock the last ball into the corner pocket. (Through trick photography, the ball at the corner pocket has been changed. But, rest assured, I successfully completed the trick each time.)

pocket. On its way to the right side pocket, ball A will strike ball D, sending D into the right corner pocket at the foot of the table and making ball E in the right side pocket. At the same time, ball C will go into the left corner pocket at the foot of the table.

You ain't seen nothin' yet.

The cue ball will glance off ball A and go three cushions, ending up its run by knocking ball F into the left corner pocket at the head of the table.

If you want to add an extra little twist, place a glass, can, or bottle of your favorite beverage in the path the cue ball will take toward ball F. Then lift it out of the way as the cue ball comes rolling by.

When the applause dies down, lift the beverage in salute to a trick shot well done—and sip it down ever so smugly.

Then, like that adorable guy in the commercial, explain you were "just showin' off."

# 8

# The Art of Pool Hustling—
# And Tips on How to Defend
# Yourself Against It

If you were making a list of all-time great sports figures, it's doubtful you'd include Tuscaloosa Squirrel, the Knoxville Bear, Cornbread Red, or Fast Eddy. But they belong on your list. They're pool hustlers supreme, outstanding at their art—or, more appropriately, at their craft.

People say pool hustling is a dying art, but don't believe it. The hustlers who can't get jobs still have only one way to earn bread: find an easy mark to play pocket billiards with for money, make him a sporting offer he can't resist, let him win a few to stir his gambling blood, and then eventually walk away with all the marbles.

So beware. The hustlers are out there on the prowl—and probably waiting to prey on *you*. Which is why I'd like to share with you some of my experiences with the hustling fraternity. Perhaps knowing what to look out for will help protect you from becoming one of the hustled, whose numbers are, as the saying goes, legion.

I don't consider myself a pool hustler, at least not a pure one. The true hustler makes his living from hustling, period, but I've always had a job (I was a schoolteacher for 13 years).

A couple of times people have tried to hustle me. When I was going to college, guys who hung around pool rooms thought I was a fresh college kid who didn't know what he was doing. Well, it cost them to find out I did. You might say I "worked" my way through college via the pool table, as so many other people did.

While the professional hustler will play down his pool-playing skills, my usual technique was to walk in and say, "I'm the best; play me."

Not always, though. There were times I deliberately played below my level—in traditional hustling style—to encourage opponents to keep competing with me and to raise the ante. It wasn't uncommon for the stakes to climb from $2 a game to $100 a game.

When I was going to school in Davenport, Iowa, I used to spend all day Saturday broadening my education at a pool room in Sterling, Illinois, where six of us used to play pool for $2 a game. We'd play 12 or 13 hours straight, and I used to win quite a bit.

Then, when I went to Athens College in Athens, Alabama (1966–1968), I used to earn spending money playing pool in billiard halls down South. I remember going down to Tallahassee, Florida, specifically to play Nine-Ball with a pretty good player, a 45-year-old man who'd play anybody. We were playing for $75 a game, and I did all right.

Some people can't resist a gamble, a weakness that hustlers capitalize on. Not that I'm a candidate for Gamblers Anonymous, but there are very few things I can enjoy fully unless I gamble on them. Still, I can control myself, and so should you.

The stakes you play for can be anything, of course, and sometimes they go sky-high. The highest amount I ever heard of being bet on one game was $42,000 for a game of One-Pocket, played either in St. Louis or Kansas City between a rich contractor who must remain nameless and a pool hustler known only by his first name, Clem. When I was just out of college and on my way home, I witnessed a game of Straight Pool (played to 300 points) in Virginia for $10,000.

The most I've ever bet on a game myself was $5,000. I was

only 21 at the time and not yet champion, and I lost. But my opponent, Danny DiLiberto, eager to add to his winnings, gave me another chance, and this time I won it back.

Sure, I trembled a little when I realized how much I was betting. But the reason I risked $5,000 was that I thought I could win. My palpitations almost escalated to a heart attack when I lost. (Danny beat me 500 to about 350.)

He was nice enough to give me a chance to win back my money, not out of a sense of charity, but because he thought he could take me for another five grand. After all, he'd beaten me once.

I accepted his offer and won the rematch, 300 points to about 150.

Southerners really seem to go into big figures—thousands of dollars—playing pool. Once they've blown their wad, some pool gamblers will put up their diamond rings, their Cadillacs, a summer house, or a business—and lose.

I remember an occasion when two young fellows got into a game and one of them blew all his cash, $400 or $500. He was wearing what appeared to be a sapphire ring with two diamonds on the side, and his opponent suggested that he put up his ring against cash. The other fellow was agreeable, and the discussion turned to the matter of how much the ring was worth. The ring's owner valued it at $300. The other player scoffed, and finally they compromised at $55. They played, and the same player who'd won all the money won the ring.

But the joke was on him, because the ring was a phony, worth about $4.95. I know that for a fact, because I'm the guy who won it.

It's more common than you think for players to bet and lose such valuables as rings, cars, and homes. They're lost by players of different abilities, some of whom qualify as sharks.

Understand that there's a difference between a pool *shark* and one who *sharks*. A pool shark is a player who's an expert at the game. But sharking is another matter. You're guilty of sharking when you engage in tactics that border on the illegal or cross the bounds of what's ethical. Let's say you wave a handkerchief around your opponent's line of vision. That's sharking. It's sharking, too, if you walk in front of him while he's about to line up a shot, or if you shout across the room. In other words, when you try to distract him or break his rhythm, attention, or concentration, you're sharking him out of a shot.

I've been the victim of many of these techniques and others.

In one match my opponent went to the bathroom seven times. I'm certain he didn't have bladder problems; it was just his way of sharking me. I've never succumbed to the temptation of using sharking techniques. I feel that unless I can win legally I don't deserve to win at all.

Luther Lassiter, the former U.S. Open champion I beat for the title in 1970 and 1973, is called Wimpy, as mentioned earlier. When somebody asked him whether he sometimes ate hamburgers to psych his opponents, he said, "That wouldn't be nice and sporting, would it? Besides," he added, "psyching someone out doesn't really help you win."

Luther's entitled to his opinion, but I disagree. I feel that psyching sometimes helps, in the sense that you get your opponent upset and he misses. Rotation Slim, a well-known hustler whose specialty and slenderness gave rise to his nickname, used to go to the bathroom in the middle of the match and spend up to half an hour there, just to psych his opponent. Waiting that long for your opponent to come back, you get cold in your chair, and it has to affect your playing. Once you get used to tactics like that, they don't bother you. In a tournament the official is supposed to be on the lookout for inordinate delays.

How much of a role psyching plays in the outcome of a game may be open to question. But there's no question that hustlers will do everything possible in the realm of psyching, conning, and sharking to victimize the unsuspecting, the greedy, and even the willing lambs of the world.

So how do you protect yourself from hustlers? Here are some suggestions.

### 1. Don't gamble.

If you don't bet, you can't be hustled and you can't lose. (Actually, there's more than enough enjoyment in the game of pool without gambling.) But then again, if you don't bet, you can't win any money. And anyway, as a lover of gambling myself, I know you're not going to accept any advice not to bet.

### 2. Play (bet) only with people you know.

Television is one development that's blamed for a decline in hustling. The theory is that when people get to know what you look like, along with an idea of what you can do, there's little chance of fooling anybody into thinking you're a less skillful player than you really are.

Television notwithstanding, an established player can sometimes manage to remain anonymous. Years ago, as a college student who had already been in televised matches and had been written up in illustrated newspaper and magazine stories, I walked into a pool hall to do a little hustling. When I was through, I noticed a picture of myself on the wall. It wasn't a beware-of-this-man type of poster, just a clipping from a magazine. But luckily, they hadn't recognized me.

There's an obvious moral: be very careful with strangers. Even if they seem like great human beings, avoid playing pool with them for money. When a true hustler comes to town intent on cleaning out the yokels, he'll invest some time. He may stay two or three weeks ingratiating himself with the pool room populace.

It stands to reason that he isn't going to come in and say, "Hey, look, I'm the best in the world; I want to play." He'll quietly scout around a couple of days, maybe get some balls and play by himself. Then, really friendly, he'll get into a game and lose. He'll do more losing than winning for a week or two. But then he'll start winning, and if he's good at his trade he'll clean the town out.

### 3. Walk away after you've won, if not before.

A true hustler not only won't show he's anxious to play with you; he'll also take it easy on you when you do play. Obviously, if he whips you too readily, you won't want to play him again. So either he'll just eke out a victory over you or, more likely, he'll lose—the object being to boost your ego and entice you into additional games at higher stakes.

If you suspect you're being hustled, stop playing as soon as you can.

Common courtesy says you should finish out the game, and if it's at the early stages of the hustle, there's a good chance you'll win a couple of dollars. That's the critical moment. If you're not sure you're being hustled, it's going to be very tempting to try to win some more. But it's very important to walk away at that point. It isn't like friendly poker games where an unwritten law dictates that you give the losers a chance to recoup their losses.

Just say to the suspected hustler something like, "Thanks. I'd love to play more, but my wife's having a baby," or "Got to get to work," or whatever. You might throw in a "Maybe tomorrow we'll play some more," but in that case remember not to show up tomorrow.

Granted, if you're not *convinced* you're up against a hustler, it will take tremendous willpower not to keep playing when you think you might win more. But if he is a hustler, you've played right into his hands. After all, your greed and overconfidence are exactly what the hustler is gambling on.

### 4. Be on the lookout for hustlers.

Identifying a hustler is the first step in keeping from playing with a hustler. Unfortunately, the only foolproof way of knowing you're being hustled is to be a hustler's victim.

There are, however, some signs you can be alert to. Simply stated, if you see a guy carrying a case with a fancy cue stick in it, and he casually invites you to a "friendly game" of Nine-Ball or something similar, look out.

But, the case doesn't have to be a fancy one and, unfortunately, neither does the cue stick. As a matter of fact, when a hustler first comes into a pool hall, he's likely to use a house stick, one belonging to the establishment. Then, when the stakes are to his liking, he'll go out to his car and bring in his own. As you know, cue sticks come in either one-piece or two-piece models. It's rare for someone to carry around a one-piece because it's so long—57 inches or more—but I remember one successful hustler who carried his one-piece with him. It should have been a giveaway to his potential opponents that he was a hustler, but apparently not many were scared away.

Cue sticks range in price from about $5 for a one-piece to thousands of dollars for a two-piece. One man I know paid $5,000 for his stick, which had inlaid pearls, ivory, and diamonds. Often, when a hustler comes off a big win he'll buy a fancy cue stick decorated with ivory and pearl. One hustler will play with his fancy new cue stick a week or two, then spend the rest of the month trying to sell it because he's broke. Next month he wins big again, buys a jazzy stick, and repeats the pattern all over again.

If you do get into that friendly game the visiting pool player invites you to, there are other signs to look for. If he starts you off at $2 a game and, after you win ten games in a row, he convinces you to raise the ante to $5 a game, beware. You should have stopped playing with him by now, but if your greed got the best of you, you might have consented to higher stakes. So stop now. Don't let him raise the ante again, because once you're up to, say, $20 a game, that's when the tide would turn, and he'd clean you out.

Earl Schriver was, without a doubt, one of the greatest con men ever to grace a pool room. An older man, Earl never worked a day in his life; all he did was hustle pool.

He had the gift of gab. "You look fine today," he'd begin. "Let's fool around on the table for a couple of dollars." He'd say it so sincerely that you couldn't resist playing him for "a couple of dollars." But very quickly he'd have you betting $20 and $40 and $60.

Earl went into Cookville, a small country town in Tennessee with a population of about 1,500 (including dogs) and convinced the pool-hall denizens he couldn't play the game at all. As superb a player as he was, he proclaimed his lack of ability so smoothly that the locals believed him. They spotted him such great odds that he couldn't help but win.

After he'd won some money he'd keep talking about playing some more. "You're too good," the others would protest, but he'd accept lower odds and they'd play some more. The odds kept going down, and he kept winning, until finally he had to give *them* odds. By the time he left town he was ahead $2,000 or $3,000, and this was a place you wouldn't expect to get $15 out of.

So beware of even the *nicest* strangers.

### 5. Beat the hustler to the punch.

I don't necessarily advocate this, but on the premise that the best defense is a good offense, you can beat the hustler to the punch, in effect outhustling him at his own game. Of course, you've got to have the goods to back up your claim.

As hust*ler* or hust*lee,* you can, as I indicated earlier, use psychology to your advantage, provided you know how to use it. Don't overdo it. For example, being brash and exuding confidence can scare your opponent into believing he can't beat you, but that may also scare him away from betting with you, thus destroying your hustling *modus operandi.*

A different strategy is more effective.

Say you have the ability to back up your bravado. Consistent with basic hustling strategy, you'll still deliberately play below par to boost your opponent's confidence and lure him into bigger bets. If you proclaim, "I'm the best" and yet perform like a bum at the table, I'm going to want to play you for $1,000. If you keep missing, it pumps up your opponent's ego and gives him an inflated sense of confidence, making it that much easier to take him.

A good measure of self-confidence is a necessity to win. And when you're trying your best you might try what some of the outstanding players do to calm themselves and psych themselves into self-assurance. Never mind that these are superstitions and have nothing to do with the game. If a player believes they help him, they do help him.

One of Arthur Cranfield's superstitions is to put chalk cubes over all the diamonds along the rails of the table before he shoots. Arthur, a friend of mine and business executive who's a tournament pool player, very seldom gambles. Even when he doesn't have a bet, he gets so nervous when he plays that he constantly jumps and dances around and tries to steer the ball into the pocket with his body. In 1971, in the Tuxedo Tournament, an invitational competition in New York City, Arthur's nervousness caused him to spin around and accidentally hit the referee, the late Al Gassner, with his cue stick, knocking him out.

Richard Riggie, a very good player, always wears white socks to play, no matter what kind of clothing he has on, even with a tuxedo. He wears the socks rolled down to his ankles with a rubber band around each sock. I like to powder my hands. Some players talk to themselves, and the late Onofrio Lauri used to whistle.

Sometimes necessity dictates self-confidence. To make a trip back to college in Alabama from my home in New Jersey, I had to borrow $35, which I estimated would be just about enough to pay for some food and for tolls and gas. A blowout changed my plans. For about 100 miles I drove on the spare, which had a plug in it, but I didn't want to risk going another 500 miles or more on it, so I bought a used tire for $13. This left me with about $12 (since I'd already spent $10), which wasn't enough to get all the way to school.

So I looked for the local pool room, where I felt certain I could earn some spending money. I found one and got into a four-handed game of Nine-Ball at $2 a game. I wasn't trying to hustle anybody, but I lost the first five games and so was down to my last couple of dollars. (This is no cop-out, but in a four-hand game of Nine-Ball you draw for the order of play, and sometimes you don't get a chance to shoot. Also, if you're shooting for, say, the 5-ball and another ball is in the way, you have to bank for it, a very difficult accomplishment.)

If I lost the next game, I'd have to borrow a dime to call somebody to wire me money. But, as it turned out, I won that game and more and ended up with more than $50.

You can be *over*confident, too. I've lost to 12-year-old kids I thought I could beat blindfolded. And as I mentioned earlier, there was the time I needed just one point to win a Tournament of Champions, played in Chicago at a country club before a small invited audience and designed especially for television. A ball was only about four inches from the pocket. I hurried to make it and blew the shot. I was 17 at the time, and I just fainted dead away on the table. I was revived about ten seconds later. It was an eternity until the TV cameras were reloaded with film. Then my opponent, after lining up and lining up the shot, blew it, too. With a new life, I took my time and scored.

**6. It's not so much how you PLAY the game, but how you MAKE the game.**

Whether you're playing a simple friendly game for nothing but the satisfaction of winning or a friendly game for money, or out-and-out hustling, this is one vital principle to keep in mind. Let me explain.

Aside from laying odds, there are many different ways to handicap a game to equalize matters for players of different abilities. In a game of straight pool we might agree that I'd have to score 100 to win, while only 25 would be enough for you to take it. Or in Nine-Ball you could win by sinking any of four different balls, while only one (the 9-ball) would win for me. And so on. These might be reasonable handicaps. But no matter by how much one player outclasses another, he can outsmart himself by giving away too large a handicap.

Even if I were ten times the player you are, if you needed just five points to win in straight pool, and I had to score 100, you'd probably beat me, because the odds were so lopsided—and even the best players are likely to miss before making 100.

In handicapping, don't take anybody for granted. Even among top-notch pro players, a lot of haggling goes on about handicaps, which is one reason a man with patience has the advantage. He'll just sit and wait until you give in to him.

Haggling over handicaps isn't done in tournaments, but suppose the player generally considered to be about 25th in the country came to visit me in the Four Seasons, a pool parlor in Metuchen, New Jersey. I'm currently regarded as one of the country's top pool players, so we'd dicker back and forth. I'd try to give him the least number of points possible, none if I could get away with it, while he'd try to get me to give the maximum. He'd probably egg me on with such statements as, "You're the champion, and you've got to play." We'd probably compromise.

Against the fellow ranked fifth in the nation I wouldn't have to give away any points, because it's a known fact the number-four or number-five player can beat number one on a given day, though more often than not the top player will come out the winner. The reason the lesser player can win is the element of luck, which accounts for 10 to 20 percent of the game. With players so closely matched, the lesser player who's lucky that day can defeat the less fortunate top-rated player.

With the right handicap, almost any good player can beat another, which reinforces what we've been saying: that a good game *maker* can beat a good game *player.*

On this point, you can certainly learn from the experts. Some players simply won't compete unless they've "got their handcuffs on"—or, put another way, they lock you up so you can't win. What all this jargon means is that I wouldn't play you unless we played a game that I *knew* I could win. That's why I'll try to make the game Straight Pool, because I'm so good at it.

Here, too, ability to hold out in negotiations is important. Even a bigger gift than his gift of gab was Earl Schriver's patience—his ability to wait and wait until he got *his* game. He was an ace at One-Pocket and Nine-Ball, so if anyone he'd scouted as a ripe hustling prospect offered to play him in Straight Pool, he'd politely but firmly decline and hold out until the other man agreed to one of Earl's specialties.

Other successful pool players share that quality, that ability to hold out.

Two players in Virginia, well known to the hustling fraternity but otherwise preferring to remain anonymous, play for as much as $1,000 a game for Straight Pool. They're not hustlers, but they know their way around a pool table. Hustlers go to try to hustle them, but they're good enough and smart enough to get enough of a handicap to hold their own against the hustlers.

Then what attracts the hustlers? The prospect of winning hundreds and hundreds of dollars. So appealing is that green these men flash at them that the hustlers can barely contain themselves. Because of the hustlers' money lust, the hosts work the handicapping so that *they,* not the hustlers, win.

You've seldom seen dickering like what goes on at tournaments in which all the great hustlers—Tuscaloosa Squirrel, Cornbread Red, and all the rest—get together in a room and try to maneuver each other into impossible situations, beginning with, "Want to play a game? What do you want to spot me?"

Tuscaloosa Squirrel, a great One-Pocket player known from pool room to pool room across the country, especially in the South, comes, obviously, from Tuscaloosa. He's very small and, let's face it, resembles a furry creature who goes nuts over acorns. That hasn't hurt his hustling career a bit.

Knoxville Bear, from Knoxville, Tennessee, is a big husky guy who's probably the greatest in the world at banking a pool ball.

Cornbread Red is a red-faced redhead from the South, who thrives on cornbread. He's still earning his (corn)bread from his specialty, Nine-Ball.

All the name hustlers are quick talkers who try to goad you into giving them handicaps.

Unfortunately, the hustlers don't confine their activities to playing each other. They're all over, even in your neighborhood pool hall—looking to make shark bait out of you.

Let's review how to defend yourself.

Bet only with people you know. Don't play with friendly strangers, no matter how cordial they act or how much they seem to be an easy mark. Make the game you play something you can win and the handicap one you can reasonably live with—and win with.

If you suspect you're being hustled, stop playing. If necessary, do some hustling of your own. Use psychology to your advantage, either to convince your opponent he hasn't a chance or the opposite, that he can eat you up alive.

## DON'T INVEST IN A HUSTLER

If you ever get the urge to back a pool player with your own money, in other words, stake him in a match, get rid of that urge at all costs.

It's one thing to make side bets on a player whose ability and reputation you trust. But to risk your money (hard-earned or otherwise) as his backer, on the chance of only a limited return, is close to financial suicide. Not only that; it's not safe. Here's how it works.

A pool player, inevitably a hustler (a jobless guy who makes his bread exclusively from pool) will ask you to bankroll him. The deal is that, if he wins, you get your investment back, plus 50 percent of the winnings. He keeps the other half. If he loses— well, at least you had some excitement for the money you lost.

In other words, you're left holding the chalk, because the risk is entirely yours, while the hustler you're backing has nothing to lose but his pride.

If you lose, you lose everything; if you win, you stand to make only 50 percent on your investment. Compare this to making a side bet, where you keep all of what you win, and backing doesn't make sense.

So why do people become backers? They feel so certain that their man will win that they welcome the chance of raking in some "sure" money, even if it is only half of the amount they risked. Maybe it's just that they're flattered that a sharp pool player has selected them as a potential "partner."

If you saw the movie *The Hustler,* you'll recall that George C. Scott played the part of Paul Newman's backer, a suave, sophisticated character.

Real-life backers, who come from all walks of life, think they're shrewd men of the world, but a lot of them are really naive, not half as smart as the players who con them into becoming backers. They often end up being hustled by the hustlers they're financing.

For example, let's suppose the hustler's opponent has demonstrated a small edge in ability at the pool table. The potential backer, figuring the hustler has purposely been playing a little sub-par to lure the other player into going for higher stakes, allows himself to be convinced he should back the hustler. But, as it turns out, the truth is that the other man *is* better, and the backer loses his investment. The hustler? He's lost just another match, but not a cent of his own money.

If you back a small-time hustler, you're really sticking your neck out, because of unreliability.

The real low-life among hustlers may even dump games. Let's

say one of these disreputable characters manages to con you into backing him for $5,000. If that's his plan, he'll keep the score close to make it appear legit, but he'll lose. Later, in secret, he and the guy he let beat him split *your* $5,000.

Of course, this happens only rarely, and the creep who is guilty of that kind of crooked caper is branded for life as the lowest of the low, but that doesn't help you recoup your money. You may learn from the incident, but it's an awfully costly lesson.

Obviously, a backer is very vulnerable, unless he backs a pool player who's not only honest but who seldom loses.

I've had people back me, and I'm happy to say I've never lost money for a backer over a long period of time. But I still don't recommend it.

To their credit, most backers are sufficiently well-heeled that they can afford to lose. Some players have more than one backer—I saw four or five people put up $20,000 to $30,000 for one match in a billiards club in the Midwest. That's a lot of cabbage, even for a sure thing.

You might well ask why, if a hustler has a very soft match, one he knows he can't lose, he needs a backer at all. In the case of an honest player, it's probably because, like most hustlers, he made a big killing at the pool table one day, then blew it the next afternoon at the track. So, needing to put down his stake for this match before it begins, he's got to find someone to back him with cash.

Usually, a backer is a big-time gambler, someone who'd bet on which ant is going to get to a bread crumb first. It's fine to be that much of a chance-taker for money, but when you're in a deal where you're risking 100 percent to win 50 percent, you're going about your gambling the wrong way. And that's what backing involves in pool, unless you can negotiate a sweeter percentage for yourself, which is unlikely.

Pool is great to gamble on. Just make sure you don't cut your money-making potential in half by backing a hustler.

Above all, enjoy your pool *playing*—but caution: play, and bet only as directed.

# Index